CREATIVE
STORYTELLING

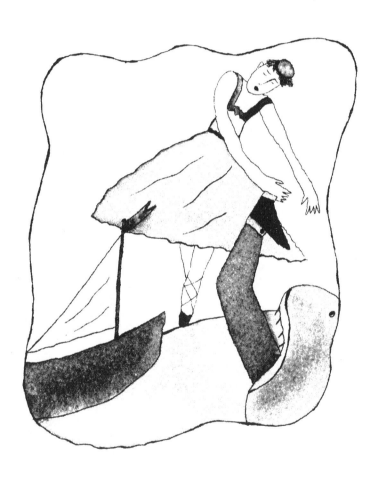

CREATIVE STORYTELLING

Choosing, Inventing, and Sharing Tales for Children

BY JACK MAGUIRE

Illustrations by Dale Gottlieb

Produced by The Philip Lief Group, Inc.

○ **YELLOW MOON PRESS** ○
P. O. Box 1316
Cambridge, Massachusetts 02238
(617) 776 - 2230

The Philip Lief Group, Inc.
319 East 52nd Street
New York, NY 10022

ISBN: 0-938756-35-4

TO MY PARENTS

CONTENTS

INTRODUCTION:
The Purposes and Values of Telling Stories
to Children   11

1 STORIES AND STORYTELLING   25
Origins and Traditions of Storytelling ◼ Past and
Present Storytellers

2 TYPES OF STORIES   47
Formula Tales ◼ Fables and Parables ◼ Fairy Tales
Folktales ◼ Myths ◼ Legends ◼ Realistic
Adventures ◼ Your Type of Story

3 FINDING STORIES FOR
DIFFERENT LISTENERS   73
Entering the World of the Child ◼ Stories that Appeal to
Children of Different Ages and Interests

4 REMEMBERING AND
ADAPTING STORIES   97
Memory Techniques for Mastering Stories ◼ Giving a
Story Your Own Style ◼ Revising Stories to Suit the
Listener and the Occasion ◼ Keeping Records of Stories

5 CREATING YOUR OWN STORIES   121
Stories You Already Know ◼ Capitalizing on Your Own
Experience, Observations, and Imagination ◼
Fashioning Story Ideas, Plots, Characters, and
Environments ◼ Creative Variations in Storytelling

6 TELLING STORIES   149

Choosing a Good Time for Storytelling ▬ Creating a
Positive Atmosphere ▬ Using Vocal Tone, Pace, and
Rhythm to Stimulate the Listener's Interest ▬ Beginning
and Ending a Story

7 BEYOND STORYTELLING   175

Puppetry ▬ Drawing ▬ Games ▬ Creative Writing
Music ▬ Poetry ▬ Excursions ▬ Making Tapes

AFTERWORD
Storytelling and Environmentalism

CREATIVE STORYTELLING

INTRODUCTION

"All twenty-five tin soldiers were exactly alike with one exception, the last one—he only had one leg. There just wasn't enough tin left over to finish him. Nevertheless, he stood as tall and as proud on one leg as the others did on two. Indeed, he was the one soldier out of all of them who actually became famous."

Throughout my life the image of Hans Christian Andersen's steadfast tin soldier has remained with me, working a quiet and special magic. When I need reassurance that it is not foolish to yearn for the unattainable, I still find myself remembering the tin soldier's love for the paper ballerina, who also balanced on only one leg. When I need courage to face difficult times alone and unappreciated, I often think of the tin soldier braving the storm-drenched gutter in his paper boat. But usually what triggers the image in my mind is a chance event that has no direct bearing on whatever themes can be drawn from the plot of the story. It has come to me when I have watched my father engrave heart-shaped lockets at county fairs and has given me a particular affection for the tin woodsman in Frank L. Baum's *The Wizard of Oz*. In this respect, the image is a touchstone for me: something around which memories gather, sensations are generated, and ideas are spun.

Storytelling is a uniquely powerful way of providing children with such life-enhancing mental images. Passed along from person to person in a natural, easygoing manner, the stuff of stories frees the imagination and stretches one's capacity for feeling joy and sorrow, sympathy and hope. Recollection of the first time I heard "The Steadfast Tin Soldier," on a cement stoop around the corner from my parents' apartment, inspired me to write this book on storytelling. Other stories and storytelling experiences also played their part: among them my grandmother's reminiscences of learning to drive a car, my minister's account of Jacob's ladder, my mother's renditions of Kipling's *Jungle Stories*, my grandfather's explanation

11

of the meaning of *mazeltov,* and my uncle's saga of how Glenn
Cunningham overcame severe leg injuries to become a track star.

A good way to begin motivating your own storytelling efforts is
to relax over the next few days and summon back favorite mental
images from the stories that were told to you when you were a
child. Stories popularized in print, film, illustrations, music, and
videotape may be the easiest to recall—stories such as "Cinderella,"
the birth of Jesus, the adventures of Daniel Boone, "Beauty and the
Beast," "The Legend of Sleepy Hollow," "Casey at the Bat," "Jack
and Jill," "Little Miss Muffet." But in addition to these stories, try
to remember stories that were more intimate to the teller or to
yourself, the listener. They may be family legends, made-up tales
about a boy or a girl much like you as a kid, or homespun yarns
about why the grass is green or what happens when you lose a
tooth. They may be visions of different lives, times, or worlds that
were brought to you by people outside the family—a neighbor, a
friend of your parents, a playmate, a teacher, an entertainer, a
doctor.

This book will help you be a transmitter of stories—a storyteller.
Although one chapter discusses reading stories aloud, the book is
primarily concerned with simply sharing a story with a child, or
with a group of children, where you can enjoy eye contact, freedom
from distraction, and mutual enchantment.

Whether you sit on moonlit Darth Vader sheets, gazing into the
eyes of one small child, or stand facing a crowd of children in a
brightly lit hall, you know instinctively when you hear the words
"tell me a story" that you are being offered a magic opportunity.
For as long as humans have enjoyed the power of speech, storytelling has enabled child and adult to come together and refresh
themselves. From the child's point of view, it is a privileged
opportunity to observe an adult closely and positively and build
new understanding, appreciation, and trust for what too often
appears to be an alien breed of puzzling and capricious giants. From
the adult's point of view, it is an excellent means of tapping one's
personal genius and of recapturing a child's sense of wonder and
play. In fact, making a habit of sharing stories with children can give
you a whole new life by enhancing your presentation skills and
creativity in general and by strengthening your bond with children
in particular.

Since the 1970s many factors have combined to threaten children's emotional, intellectual, and social well-being and to make the need for storytelling all the more critical. More and more households have only one resident parent; and among two-parent households, a greater and greater percentage of both parents work. This has inevitably resulted in less available time for parent-child encounters, which has deprived many children of the type of dependable and nonthreatening listening experiences with adults that storytelling offers. Even more alarming is how many of these children lack sufficient reassurance that adults know how they feel, think, and dream. Storytelling has a unique way of consoling, healing, and reviving the child who is eager for word pictures to help express what he or she perceives, for hero figures and role models, and for creative insights into the motives and patterns of human behavior.

But storytelling has an even more potent value. Children today are immersed in an overtly visual world of television, computers, and video arcades, which is having a disastrous effect on their abilities to listen, to think in words, and to exercise the "mind's eye." Even reading aloud to children is frequently directing them to concentrate on what they can see: the book that contains the text of the story. Noting the rapid decline of language skills over the past two generations, child psychologists and educators are now actively championing storytelling as an ideal method of influencing a child to associate listening with pleasure, of increasing a child's attention span and retention capacity, of broadening a child's vocabulary, and of introducing a child to the symbolic use of language. The specific educational and social benefits of storytelling from the child's point of view are numerous and well documented. In addition to increasing a child's vocabulary, concentration, and ability to think symbolically and metaphorically, they include:

- building a child's sensitivity to various forms of syntax, diction, and rhetoric;
- helping a child to recognize patterns in language and in human experience;
- stimulating a child's overall powers of creativity;
- providing a child with problem-solving and decision-making exercises;
- strengthening a child's capacity to form objective, rational, and practical evaluations;

- assisting a child to develop skills in dialogue and cooperative interpersonal behavior;
- familiarizing a child with the symbols, artifacts, and traditions that are part of his or her own cultural heritage;
- introducing a child to the symbols, artifacts, and traditions that characterize the cultural heritages of others with whom he or she shares the world.

Most important of all, a storytelling session in itself is a delightful social exchange. It not only unites teller and listener but also links both of them to the universe of human drama. When you tell stories to children, you lead them to realms beyond the limited circles of their own daily existence and give them sudden flashes of the possibilities of life they would not otherwise receive. In turn, you are given a point of access to your listeners themselves and to the world of childhood you once inhabited but may have forgotten.

An incident that occurred almost ten years ago brought this fact home to me. It involves Winnie Carlson, who was three years old at the time. You might say that Winnie and I are spiritual relatives: Her mother is also a godparent of several of my godchildren. One night I was at a party given by the Carlsons. When it was time for Winnie to go to bed, she asked me if I would tell her a story, and I agreed. Climbing the stairs to her bedroom, I felt nervous. I was a bachelor and had not been around many children for quite a while, due to the academic and social demands of graduate school and college teaching. I could not even recall the last time I had told a story to a child. Entering her bedroom, I noticed a picture of a giraffe. It rekindled my old storytelling instincts and I spun a tale of Sparky the Giraffe, a sort of Rudolph-the-Red-Nosed-Reindeer story, transposed to Africa. Days later I drew pleasure from thoughts of that story and of Winnie and of the jump I had made back into the perspective of a child. It made me eager to see Winnie again and, I later learned, made her eager to see me. I had created a new friendship through storytelling, and I had also rediscovered a part of myself that I had lost without being aware of it.

Since that event I have kept track of my storytelling experiences and the procedures and techniques I have found helpful. They form the basis for this book, along with many interviews with professional and amateur storytellers and extensive research into childhood development, the art of storytelling, and children's literature.

This book is addressed to anyone who wants to tell stories to children or who already tells stories to children and is on the lookout for fresh approaches. You may be a parent who needs to become more comfortable with the idea of storytelling and who would like some tips about preparing to tell stories as well as actually delivering them. You may be a frequent visitor to households with children who seeks to make those visits more memorable and constructive. You may be a teacher who is searching for ways to apply storytelling successfully in the classroom. You may be a counselor, a day-care-center worker, a librarian, a psychologist, a physician, a member of the clergy, a babysitter . . . or, more to the point, you may simply be curious about children and/or stories.

In the process of planning and writing this book, I had conversations with all kinds of potential readers, and the book eventually took shape around their concerns. Several key issues arose again and again. As a means of introducing you to what this book covers, I believe it would be useful to confront each of these issues, briefly, at this point. I have phrased some of the issues as questions and some as attitudes, depending on how they were most frequently communicated to me.

Is this a book about telling fairy tales?

Creative Storytelling does discuss fairy tales but also many other types of stories, such as formula tales, fables and parables, folktales, myths, legends, and realistic adventure stories. This book offers you much more, however, than a discussion of tales for children. It is a practical guide that will tell you how to become a more effective storyteller, regardless of the type of story you tell. After reading this book, you will be able to:

- understand and appreciate the value and tradition of storytelling;
- recognize the fundamental elements in every effective children's story;
- distinguish among the characteristics and purposes of different types of stories for children;
- select stories that will appeal to a specific child, based on his or her interests, age, and developmental needs;
- locate children's stories that you and your listener will enjoy;

- create your own entertaining children's stories;
- remember children's stories that you read, hear, or create easily and accurately;
- adapt children's stories to fit individual listeners and storytelling occasions;
- identify and set up good storytelling opportunities;
- deliver stories confidently and successfully;
- use storytelling as a gateway to a wide range of other creative activities that you and a child can enjoy together, such as puppetry, drawing, games, creative writing, music, poetry, and excursions.

Technically, a fairy tale is a story in which the plot turns on the magical intervention of a fairy; but in common usage it has come to mean any story involving magical occurrences or nonrealistic characters, like talking animals. It has even accumulated pejorative connotations, being freely associated with "a lie" or, in the arena of storytelling, with "entertainment for babies who don't know any better." In light of this, I normally avoid the label "fairy tale" altogether when talking with children, in case it may cause confusion.

One of the main purposes of this book is to help you realize that each individual story stands on its own. There are not many clear-cut distinctions among different categories of stories, no fixed story patterns that have to be followed, and no established criteria that must be met in order for a given story to be successful in its own right.

Effective, time-tested patterns for your own stories certainly exist among the basic plots or actual written versions of fairy tales and other types of stories. But when you tell a story to a child, you will inevitably be adapting it and perhaps even turning it into an entirely different type of story. This book is designed to give you confidence in your own powers of observation, translation, and communication.

A story, after all, takes its final shape in the telling. When you tell a story to a child, you are not giving a recitation or performing a dramatic monologue. You are sharing your own account of a series of interesting story events. You need no rigid superstructure. A good story can be full of borrowings, spur-of-the-moment changes, interruptions, pauses, and exclamatory bursts. Ideally, a story will be somewhat loosely woven, with room for the listener to allow his or her imagination to roam freely—and fill in the gaps. Like the best of homemade crafts, a well-told story is simple. The form and materials may be familiar, but it is the individual care and personality of the maker that gives it its character.

What are the basic storytelling techniques?

The most important step is to prepare for storytelling. One aspect of this preparation involves easy research that can provide you with a great deal of fun. Read stories written for children. Observe children and note what interests them. Look more closely at the world around you and keep track of story ideas. Listen to other people—children and adults—when they tell stories. Check out storytelling records and television programs for children. Another aspect of this preparation is to ensure that individual storytelling sessions are set up properly. Make storytelling a special treat rather than springing it on your listener. Children love rituals, and there are many simple devices for putting both you and your listener in a particularly receptive mood for storytelling.

Another key technique is to be relaxed and natural in your delivery of a story. Imagine you are carrying on a conversation with a friend and suddenly that friend says, gleefully, "Oh, tell me all about that!" Storytelling does offer you such an ideal listening situation. Both you and your listener can appreciate storytelling as an oasis of relief from everyday concerns: You are not burdened with having to be factual and your listener is not burdened with having to retain your words and respond to them as if they were commands or required information. When a child agrees to hear a story, you are more or less receiving a blank check. Be expansive and don't worry about special gestures, voices, or vocabulary. Maintain eye contact with your listener and speak slowly and distinctly and you will almost certainly command his or her attention.

A chief element in being natural and relaxed when telling stories is to give yourself fully to the spirit of the moment. Don't be distracted by attempting to repeat a story exactly the way you remember it or by trying to fashion sentences correctly as if you were reading a story aloud. I came across one of the best illustrations of a relaxed and natural storytelling technique in a biography of Hans Christian Andersen written by his longtime friend and patron, Edvard Collin. It is worth quoting here.

> In many of the circles to which he paid daily visits were little children with whom he connected himself; he told them stories which he had partly made up for the occasion, and partly taken from familiar fairy tales; but whether the tales he told were of his own invention or borrowed, his manner of telling them was so exclusively his own and so vivid, that the children were enchanted. He himself enjoyed having a chance to give his humor full play, his speech came in an unobstructed stream, richly provided with gestures to fit. He put life into even the driest sentence; he did not say: "The children climbed up into the wagon and then they rode away," but: "Then they climbed up into the wagon, good-by, father, good-by, mother, the whip cracked, snap, snap and away they went, hey, will you really pull there!" Those who have heard him read his fairy tales later on can only form a weak notion of the strange vitality his delivery had in the midst of a circle of children. (*H.C. Andersen and the Collin Family*, 1882, as quoted in Fredrik Book's *Hans Christian Andersen*, 1962: University of Oklahoma Press, p. 193.)

I don't know any good stories and storytelling
does not come naturally to me.

This book will assist you in locating stories, or story models, and in remembering those stories for later storytelling sessions. The text also includes many capsule versions of stories you can use without having to refer to other sources. But most likely you already do know more stories than you realize. Stories of characters in your own family or circle of friends; stories from television shows, movies, plays, musical comedies, and operas you have seen; stories about famous people, places, or events that are part of your cultural heritage—all of these can provide material for stories to tell children.

You may lack experience in storytelling, but it is my firm belief that the storytelling instinct is an innate fixture in the human psyche and that everyone is capable of developing that instinct and becoming a good storyteller. Try this experiment: Think of a police officer laughing on a raft. Chances are you will immediately begin weaving a story, albeit on a semiconscious level, to fit, explain, or elaborate that image. I have conducted this experiment with hundreds of creative writing students over the years, using randomly distributed characters, activities, and settings. No one has ever had difficulty producing a story, and no two stories have ever been quite the same. All that is needed is the stimulus.

Each of us goes through much the same semiconscious story-weaving process whenever we hear a joke, or take careful notice of a stranger, or study a photograph. The trick is to bring that automatic facility to a conscious level. This book is meant to make you more aware of your own natural storymaking talent and enable you to exercise that talent for the purpose of telling stories to children.

I don't have much time to give to storytelling.

Some people who expressed this concern literally do not have much time in their daily schedules to spend with children. Storytelling is an especially flexible activity—one that you can fit into any time frame. Individual storytelling sessions can last anywhere from two minutes to an hour or more. Storytelling can be conducted on a daily basis or only on special occasions. Storytelling can greatly enhance the quality of time that you already spend with children, replacing some of the time taken up by less rewarding and less intimate activities, like watching television or playing with toys.

Usually when people made this comment, however, they were apprehensive about the amount of time it might take to locate, develop, and master a repertoire of stories and, through experience, evolve into successful storytellers. I have organized this book so that it can accommodate a wide range of ambitions. It is possible to read this book and begin immediately to tell stories to children confidently and effectively. If you want to pursue a more formal program for developing your storytelling skills after you have finished this book, I have included a one-month action plan that you can customize to fit your particular situation.

How do I know what stories a child will like?

Storytelling is a cooperative venture: Both the teller and the listener play roles. Laura Simms, a storyteller for the American Museum of Natural History and the New York Foundation of the Arts, has a beautiful way of describing this partnership: "Storytelling is like sailing on a thin silk thread. I'm the ferryman. My listeners make the scenery." If you enjoy a story, if you really have a personal affection for it, the odds are very strong that your listener will enter into the spirit of the story with you and enjoy it too.

If a child doesn't like a story, he or she will let you know, and without making any fuss you can change the story itself or switch to a new story. This book contains advice for handling such situations smoothly. More important, it also provides you with descriptions of a wide range of story types and guidelines for choosing specific stories to fit different age groups, personalities, and circumstances.

I'm concerned about the psychological effect certain stories may have on children: making them believe things that aren't true, or frightening them, or exposing them to negative stereotypes.

One of the unique virtues of storytelling is that it enables both teller and listener to take time out from the real world. Every child knows that stories are "make-believe." Even stories based on true events are accepted as playthings—items of entertainment that are valued precisely because they require no specific application to day-by-day existence.

"Make-believe truths" are crucial in a child's psychological development. Whether or not they are presented in the context of storytelling, a child is bound to form personal fantasies about everything he or she experiences, on both conscious and unconscious levels. We can't expect children to deal rationally with all the pressures of growing up, which include recognizing the good and bad in themselves as well as in others. They are well aware that life is not always pleasant; and unless this fact is acknowledged in some manner that speaks to their imaginations, they are apt to feel frustrated and insecure.

Storytelling gives children more scope for working out their dreamlike perceptions of life, for symbolically confronting its myriad opportunities and difficulties. It equips them with tools—images and words—that they can use to test their intuition and powers of judgment; and it safely and gently introduces topics that can later be discussed openly outside of the privileged world of storytelling.

For these reasons, I do not believe as a rule that all stories for children must have happy endings or need to be sanitized by removing incidents of violence or passages that are perceived as containing potentially troublesome "hidden messages." Children's stories are simple things. They are not sermons, pronouncements, philosophical tracts, or training instruments. They are action-oriented narratives of events; their main appeal rests in the fact that they do not tell anyone how to think or behave or what is actually going to happen in day-to-day life.

If you as the would-be storyteller are automatically turned off by a specific story you have heard or read, you are liable to be uncomfortable telling it to a child, so it is wise not to do so. I personally feel that examining an individual children's story to determine whether or not it contains elements that may be construed as racist, sexist, or ethnocentric is not necessary for the purposes of constructive and responsible storytelling. I do not feel that children are likely to make such inferences regarding children's stories on their own. Children's stories do not pretend to portray the real world and the characters in them are too narrowly developed to be mistaken for real people.

Our behavior around children in daily life determines whether or not they develop non-racist, non-sexist, and non-ethnocentric attitudes. Children, I believe, look to stories for completely different, more personalized reasons. By eliminating a good story on the grounds of a hypothetical interpretation that can be read into it by an adult, we, as storytellers, risk robbing children of their chance to experience the story in their own private way and test their own individual feelings.

One parent with whom I spoke expressed concern over the number of children's stories featuring passive maidens waiting for men to rescue them and wicked stepmothers bent on preventing their stepchildren from realizing fortune and happiness. It is undeniable that several of the currently most popular children's tales, such as "Cinderella," "Snow White," and "Sleeping Beauty," contain both of these features; but I believe that to attribute this fact to any sexist bias in society is to miss the point entirely.

There are valid psychological reasons why these stories have remained favorites with boys as well as girls for such a long period. of time. Children and adolescents, especially females, are forced by their culture (the "stepparent" they never chose) to remain relatively passive as far as their innermost desires are concerned. It is a situation—not a character trait—that is "safely" acknowledged and condemned by these tales, and a situation that begins to be rectified when the heroines assert their independence (Cinderella going to the ball, Snow White fleeing the castle, and Sleeping Beauty exploring the forbidden room with the spinning wheel).

There are also historical reasons why these stories took the shape they did and why they are now important metaphors for the human condition in a previous era. Unmarried household members in the Middle Ages—regardless of sex—were compelled to live at home under the governance of their parents until they formed their own family households. The unmarried prince is scarcely more free to do as he wishes than Cinderella is; and for every story of a passive woman waiting for a man to release her from entrapment, there is a story of a passive man waiting for a woman to release him from entrapment (for example, "The Frog Prince," "East of the Sun and West of the Moon," and "Beauty and the Beast"). Reluctant stepmothers in the Middle Ages were a common and tragic result of the great number of mothers who died during childbirth; and present-day, real-life stepchildren are highly unlikely to assume that their stepmothers are wicked by nature, based on the bizarre caricatures of medieval stepmothers they find in these stories. Brief remarks about historical conditions relevant to a story, offered as interesting facts rather than explanations of the story's contents, can help clarify such matters to your listeners if you genuinely feel they need the clarification.

But leaving aside these reasons for the hold such stories have over the human imagination and skipping over whatever other reasons can be uncovered (some of which may lie in the psyche of Walt Disney, who did so much in recent history to promote "Cinderella," "Snow White," and "Sleeping Beauty"), it certainly is distressing to think that a child would be exposed only to this kind of subject matter—particularly so for a stepmother! The solution lies in offering children a wide variety of stories. There are plenty of tales around (and plenty you can create) about males or females, mothers or fathers, stepmothers or stepfathers, blacks or whites or reds or yellows, who are good or bad, active or passive, wise or foolish, helpful or helpless.

This book will help you to locate, adapt, and create stories that express whatever kind of situation you desire. There is no good reason to deny a child the opportunity of hearing stories that are part of his or her cultural inheritance (such as "Cinderella," "Rapunzel," "Br'er Rabbit and the Tar Baby," or "Huckleberry Finn") because of adult-world theories about their present-day relevance. There is every good reason, however, to supplement these stories with other stories that present contrasting subject matter. One excellent recently published source for such counterbalancing children's stories, as well as for story ideas, is Letty Cottin Pogrebin's *Stories for Free Children* (McGraw-Hill, 1982).

I'm worried about a child not understanding many of the words I may use in telling a story.

Not only is a child's listening vocabulary far greater than his or her speaking vocabulary, but a child also has much more tolerance for ambiguity than an adult has. A child's mind will be busy spinning its own sense of things as you are telling a story; in fact, you may say that a storytelling experience from the child's point of view is one of guided daydreaming. Suppose you were relating this passage to a child: "Oh, it was an inviting barn! In the loft the sun was shining on the hay and you could sniff clover in the atmosphere." The child may actually retain only the words "barn . . . shining . . . hay . . . sniff clover," not certain of what is meant by "inviting," "loft," and "atmosphere," and still be greatly satisfied with the image you have produced.

Storytelling can be a delightful medium for introducing a child to new words or even just new sounds: details for the child to cogitate after the story is finished. Above all, you want the story to flow smoothly and you don't want to inhibit yourself by worrying over individual words. If the context of the word does not indicate the meaning of the word clearly enough, trust the child to ask you about it, at which time you can offer a short explanation.

How can I overcome my "stage fright" about telling a story?

An element of nervousness or stage fright is present in every spoken encounter you have with another person. Recognizing that storytelling is one of the least intimidating types of encounters helps eliminate that nervousness—you don't have any points you must make or any specific topics you must address, and you have a captive audience, one that sees you as a magically superior being. This book is meant to stimulate your interest in storytelling, so that you will be more motivated to initiate storytelling opportunities; it will also present you with numerous tips for preparing both you and your listener to relax and enjoy the storytelling session.

A story told to a child is truly, in the words of Lewis Carroll, a "love gift." More than that, it is a natural extension of the creative talents that enabled you to cope with childhood and adolescence and mature into a responsible adult. *Creative Storytelling* is designed to help you make the most of those talents in order to improve your own life and the lives of those who look up to you for guidance.

CHAPTER ONE

STORIES AND STORYTELLING

As a child, I was fascinated by the concept that all human beings are descended from Adam and Eve. It thrilled me to think that my newly acquired, highly cherished playmate was in a sense a relative, maybe my thirty-first cousin, and that the world of peoples—incalculably vast and varied to my young mind—was, in fact, a *family* of peoples.

We can experience the exact same sense of awe and delight when we begin to study storytelling. Not only can we be impressed with how ancient many of our favorite stories are, and how strong the family resemblance is between these stories and tales from widely divergent cultures, but also we can be moved by the vigor and beauty of the oral tradition that gave birth to stories, refined them, passed them from one part of the world to another, and ensured their survival over millennia of human experience. Hearing a story today, I imagine all the voices behind it: the chain of sound and life that links that story to other stories, all the way back to the original stories men and women created out of a compulsion to share their personal vision of the human drama with others.

Throughout the ages and in all parts of the world, the same themes, plots, and characters have been ceaselessly recast in the

27

form of spoken stories, each new telling retaining much of the imagery and style of the past but freshened by the language and perceptions of the teller and living anew in the mind of the listener. The history of the story that most of us know as "Cinderella" offers a striking example of this process.

For centuries "Cinderella" has been one of the most popular folktales, perhaps because it deals with such essential human concerns as sibling rivalry, the parent-child relationship, the yearning for appreciation and success, and the trauma of becoming an adult. Different versions of it appear in Chinese literature from the ninth century (where the beauty of the heroine's small feet is emphasized), in Icelandic sagas from the tenth century, and in the recorded legends of France, Austria, Italy, England, Poland, Russia, and central Africa from more recent times.

Despite its popularity, I did not particularly enjoy "Cinderella" when I was a child. I can't say why this was so. Maybe it was because I was overexposed to it: Walt Disney's immensely successful movie version of "Cinderella" made its first appearance then, there was a Rodgers & Hammerstein television production, and we staged our own theatrical version at my elementary school. My attitude toward "Cinderella" suddenly changed after I heard a rendition of the story I had never before encountered during my first visit to Scotland. The storyteller was a student at the University of Glasgow, and he called the main character "Aschenputtel." In his telling of the tale, Aschenputtel's father is going to a fair one day and he asks Aschenputtel and her stepsisters what gifts they would like him to bring home for them. One stepsister begs for diamonds. The other stepsister wants expensive clothes. But Aschenputtel says, "Give to me only the first branch that strokes your cheeks on your journey home." The father returns safely and presents Aschenputtel with a hazel bough. She plants it on her mother's grave. Every day when she visits the grave to talk with her mother, her tears water the bough, and it grows into a beautiful tree.

The story the student told me was not, as I'd first assumed, a Scottish version. A truly Scottish Cinderella, named "Rashin Coatie," does exist—her mother gives her a russet calf to remember her by. I later discovered that the story I had heard in Glasgow was more closely related to a Bohemian version of "Cinderella," predating the French version I knew which Walt Disney had popularized during my childhood. Whatever its origin, when I first heard the story of Aschenputtel that evening in Glasgow, all at once the Cinderella story clicked for me. I liked hearing more about the father, the mother, and the stepsisters: They seemed less like cartoons. I also felt more kinship with a Cinderella who performed private little ceremonies, because I did too. Having a better understanding of the characters, I began to look forward to telling the story. And I began to realize that exploring different versions of stories can be an immensely valuable activity for the creative storyteller.

It is also inspirational to learn how many different stories embody the same themes. In Moscow, I met a woman who told me a story about a forgotten sentinel, waiting perpetually at attention all by himself, that transmitted precisely the same commentary on perseverance and destiny that I had received from "The Steadfast Tin Soldier." On a hilltop overlooking Sun Valley, Idaho, I once swapped stories of the lives of the Roman Catholic saints with a Jew, a Mormon, a Buddhist, and a Baptist native American for stories from their own backgrounds. We were all simultaneously humbled and excited by the remarkable similarities in spiritual life qualities and ethical codes that were revealed among stories of Saint Agatha, the Catholic martyr; of Baal Shem Tov, the Hasidic leader; of Joseph Smith, who struggled to found the Church of Latter-day Saints; of Siddhartha Gautama, the Buddha; and of Tate, the Sacred Being who became a Lakota man.

Comparing stories about the same human activity that have blossomed forth in different ages and diverse parts of the globe is another way to develop an appreciation for the power of storytelling to capture and communicate the oneness of humankind. Any story I tell about hunting or chasing is certain to contain qualities I borrowed from the tales I heard at summer camp about Rock Stalls, a local land configuration into which the Miami Indians once herded game, and from the whaling yarns I listened to one black October night in a Nantucket meeting house.

You will benefit greatly in your quest to become a more creative storyteller if you give some attention to the history of stories and storytelling. The overview offered in this chapter will highlight those facts that motivate my own interest in the subject; and it will also familiarize you with the basic kinds of tales that emerged from this history and continue to be patterns for stories today. I will begin my discussion, logically enough, with a story.

How stories came to be

SPIDER AND THE BOX OF STORIES

One day a long time ago, Spider determined to visit the Lord of the Sky, Nyami, to see if he could buy the box that Nyami always kept beside him. In that box was every story in the world. Spider wove a web to the sky and when he reached Nyami's throne, he asked Nyami what he would take in exchange for the box of stories. "Bring to me a python, a leopard, a hornet, and a creature that none can see," Nyami said to Spider. "Then you may have the box."

Spider went back to his wife, Aso, and said "I must capture a python." Aso said, "Cut some vine." Spider said, "Enough! I understand." He cut some vine and took it to a python in the jungle. "Python," he said, "I am having an argument with my wife, Aso. She says this vine is shorter than you, and I say it is longer. Stretch out on this path alongside the vine and I will measure you." The python did what Spider said. Moving swiftly, Spider wrapped the vine around the python and carried him up to Nyami, who received it and said, "Three more remain."

Spider returned to Aso and said, "I must capture a leopard." Aso said, "Dig a hole." Spider said, "Enough! I understand." Spider dug a hole in the trail the leopard took to get to the water and then hid himself in the bushes. The thirsty leopard came bounding by and fell into the hole. Spider walked over to the edge and peered down. "Reach up to me so I can pull you out," he said. The leopard stood and raised his arms and Spider bound them with a vine and knocked the leopard out with a rock. He carried the leopard up to Nyami, who received it and said, "Two more remain."

Spider came home to Aso and said, "I must capture a hornet." "Get a calabash," Aso said. Spider said, "Enough! I understand." He found the gourd, hollowed it out, filled it with water, and took it to the hornet's nest. There he lifted the calabash and sprinkled some water on the nest and the rest on his head. "Hornet," Spider yelled, "the rains have come! Protect yourself and fly into this calabash where you will stay dry." The hornet flew into the calabash. Spider pushed in the stopper behind the hornet and carried the calabash up to Nyami, who received it and said, "One more remains."

Spider came back once more to Aso and said, "I must capture a creature that none can see." Aso said, "Make a doll." Spider said, "Enough! I understand." He made the doll, tying a vine to its head, so that he could move it up and down, and covering the doll's entire body with sticky dark honey. Then Spider placed the doll in front of a tree with yams in its lap and hid himself behind the tree, where he held on to the free end of the vine. A creature that no one can see came up and asked the doll, "Are these yams for me?" The doll nodded yes and the creature took the yams and ate them. "Thank you," he said to the doll. The doll did not move. "I said thank you," the creature screamed. "Answer me or I will spank you!" When he got no response for the second time from the doll, the creature began spanking it and soon he was stuck to the doll's surface. Spider carried the doll up to Nyami, who received it and said, "No more remains. The box of stories is yours."

Spider scrambled back home with the box and cried, "Come see! I have all the world's stories in this box." Aso ran up and so did the other villagers. When he had finished the story of how he got the box, Spider flung it open and all the stories leapt out and began flying everywhere. Spider caught some, Aso caught some, the villagers caught some, but the rest scattered to the four corners of the world.

Anansi, or Spider, is a favorite character of the Ashanti and other African peoples. The story you have just read is an adaptation of Paul Jordan-Smith's version of "Anansi's Box of Stories," which he, in turn, first heard from one of the most famous contemporary American storytellers, Jay O'Callahan. Were O'Callahan actually telling it to you, he would conclude, "I caught a story and this is it. If it be bitter, or if it be sweet, take some away and bring some back."

For me, "Anansi's Box of Stories" magically conveys several fundamental truths about stories and storytelling. Stories are god-given. It is human nature to desire them and to strive to possess them. They are spread all over the world, but they do have a supernatural point of origin—they are all, in a manner of speaking, from the same "box." And to possess a story, the teller must be able to master a variety of experiences—including capturing the "unseen"—and to transmit to the sky the results of that mastery, which always incorporate an element of the teller's invention with the mastered experience itself.

Men and women began telling stories long before written records of any aspect of human endeavor existed; but we can probably best understand why and how stories originated by listening to the first stories that children create for themselves. Typically, these stories are made up to accompany what the child is doing, to express how he or she feels about it, and, often, to boast about it. The stories are strongly flavored with the child's own fantastic sense of things, since the child, after all, must rely on imagination to explain what reason cannot yet grasp.

The oldest stories we can establish in any region of the world—many of them directly related to stories told in present-day primitive societies—possess these same characteristics. They are tales of physical prowess or individual contributions to important events. In successive retellings, they were no doubt given personal touches by each new storyteller, until precise names, places, and dates became uncertain and irrelevant: The stories survived on the strength of their capacity to arouse general human interest and emotion, assisted by the powers of those special people who were gifted at storytelling.

Stories of record

The oldest written version of a story we have illustrates a much greater advance in the evolution of stories: a step beyond the self-involved story to the story designed to influence the listener's behavior. It is known as "The Tale of Two Brothers" and can be found in an Egyptian papyrus dating from around 1250 B.C. In this story, a younger brother rejects the amorous advances of his older brother's wife. Frustrated and afraid that the younger brother will publicly denounce her, she tells her husband that it was the younger brother who tried to seduce her. The older brother is furious and tries to kill the younger brother, who flees, wounded, into the wilderness. The gods intervene and the truth is revealed; but the older brother's drink turns sour, which is a sign that his brother has already died. The older brother manages to find the body and revive it.

The messages imbedded in "The Tale of Two Brothers" are clear: Do not be carried away by your emotions; honor wins out in the end; it is never too late to make amends. The biblical account of Joseph and Potiphar's wife most likely derives from this story; and the kind of tale it represents, the "cautionary" tale, appears in equally ancient texts written in Chinese, Sumerian, and Sanskrit. Unfortunately, we can only speculate about how and by whom such stories were actually delivered. We do know that successive migrations of people in the centuries that followed distributed such tales throughout the Eurasian landmass, and that they were continually customized to fit different political, religious, and social ways of life.

Gradually the spoken story developed to serve a multitude of practical purposes. In some tales, the goal of entertaining and providing relief from the rigors of daily existence appears dominant. In others, we recognize the desire to immortalize ancestors or preserve memories of past experiences and customs. Tales also evolved to interpret the mysteries of nature, to honor supernatural forces, and to fulfill an aesthetic need for expressions of beauty and order. The *Iliad* and the *Odyssey* were composed from such tales over 2,700 years ago and were probably recited by illiterate storytellers for hundreds of years before they were written down. Wandering tribespeople of Israel collected and perpetuated all manner of folktales that later found their way into the Bible and, according to early Hebrew scholars, into the lost books of the Apocrypha.

By the time of the Roman Empire, storytelling was well established as a means of imparting wisdom to children. The historian Strabo makes the following comment in his *Geography* (first century A.D.):

> Man is eager to learn and his fondness for tales is a prelude to this quality. It is fondness for tales, then, that induces children to give their attention to narratives and more and more to take part in them. The reason for this is that myth is a new language to them—a language that tells them, not of things as they are, but of a different set of things. And what is new is pleasing, and so is what one did not know before, and it is just this that makes men eager to learn. But if you add to this the marvellous and the portentous, you thereby increase the pleasure, and pleasure acts as a charm to incite the learning. At the beginning we must needs make use of such bait for children.

As Roman soldiers, colonizers, and civil administrators penetrated deeper and deeper into Europe and Asia, they helped create the single most pervasive distribution of tales among different cultures the world had ever known.

After the fall of the Roman Empire, the most significant disseminators of stories were the people known as the gypsies. We can be certain of very little about their early history. They were nomadic and migrated from the East, perhaps from India, to

Europe. They possessed their own language, Romani, which seems to be derived from Sanskrit or Prakrit, but were quick to adopt new languages in the course of their travels. They claimed descent from the first pharoah of Egypt. What is indisputable is their reputation for glib tongues, dramatic flair, and a proficiency in plundering and remodeling the folklore and mythology of every region they visited. Medieval monarchs, monks, and manor lords valued the gypsies' storytelling abilities highly, but they were seldom permitted to remain in any one place for an extended length of time.

So the gypsies journeyed, following caravans of traders and leaving their tales behind them from Afghanistan to Britain, from Finland to North Africa. Soon the traffic of tales across Europe and Asia was increased by Christians engaging in the Crusades and in individual or group pilgrimages.

Storytelling: an art, a science, a way of life

While the gypsies, Crusaders, and pilgrims were wandering back and forth across Europe, two distinct disciplines of storytelling were evolving from the native Celtic tradition right next to each other in the British Isles: the Cymric school of bards in Wales and the Gaelic school of ollamhs in Ireland. By the beginning of the thirteenth century they had each achieved a degree of professionalism that has never since been equaled, attracting both scholars and would-be storytellers from all over the known world.

The Celtic schools gave to storytelling a formal structure of skill-training and performance guidelines, some of which inform techniques and ideas presented later in this book. They also equipped students not only to accumulate and retain a great number of popular stories but also to build stories spontaneously by exercising their imaginations. As a result, the Celtic tradition has provided the world with a larger and more ancient body of folktales than any other single source. Many scholars claim that the flowering of European romance ballads in the following centuries can be directly attributed to the stimulus of these schools and the infusion of the tales they preserved into the cultures of the Romance-speaking nations.

Both schools divided storytellers into ranks. In the Cymric school, the *penkerdd*, or "chief of song," held the highest rank. He was usually attached to a single household and celebrated the lives and deeds of the most ancient and the most famous Britons. He was granted a free holding of land by the king and always sat to the left of his master. Second in rank was the *barrd teulu*. He accompanied the head of the household in battle and told tales to inspire courage and valor. Farther down in rank were the apprentices, or *mabinogs*, who gave their name to the famous Welsh cycle of tales the *Mabinogion*, which were those stories that had to be known by every apprentice before he could rise to a higher rank. Often the mabinog traveled from household to household, changing teachers.

The Irish *ollamhs* were divided into nine categories, depending on their area of expertise. There were recounters of history, keepers of genealogies, poet-singers, composers of hero stories, moral and legal fabulists, rhetoricians, wits, wisdom-sayers, and tellers of mystery tales. A high-ranking ollamh maintained a retinue of twenty-four persons, some of them apprentices, and a repertoire of "seven times fifty" stories. Like a penkerdd, he was usually a fixed member of a large household or court and enjoyed high esteem within his society. According to one Irish law from this period listing the clothing due to various ranks of people, an accomplished ollamh could wear five colors, only one less than royalty.

Once a year in ancient Ireland a truce-gathering was held for all the clans at Tara, seat of the High King. Each clan brought its chief ollamh, who was required to tell a new story to the High King. If he did not have a new story, the penalty could be severe: public humiliation, physical injury, or loss of possessions. In her classic book *The Way of the Storyteller,* Ruth Sawyer relates a tale about such an event, which I will summarize here, since it has much to say symbolically about creative storytelling.

THE STORYTELLER AT TARA

One day at Tara, the High King commanded the ollamh of the clan Fianna to tell him a new story that night or he would forfeit his life. The man was desperate because he had no new tale, and it was against the law to take one from another ollamh. He said to himself, "Go and find yourself a tale or you'll never be seeing tomorrow's sun." Out he went toward the forest of Tara, followed by Bran, the Fianna hound, who was born of a woman, sired by a fairy. Suddenly a white doe sprang from a thicket and Bran began pursuing it. The ollamh raced behind them, forgetting for the moment his grave trouble. Faster and faster the three of them ran. The ollamh saw the doe change to a pigeon and take the air; then Bran changed to a falcon and flew after her. The ollamh watched them chase each other back and forth across the sky. Then the pigeon dove into a stream and became a trout, and the falcon changed into a salmon, going after the trout. Change after change occurred, the pursuer never slacking speed after the pursued, until the ollamh found himself standing in front of the queen with Bran beside him. "Teller of tales," the queen said, "proceed to the feast with a peaceful mind. Have you not now a decent story to be telling?"

This story is just one example of a run of Gaelic stories about storytellers driven by adventurousness or desperation to seek new story material. Together they constitute a cycle similar in nature to *The Thousand and One Nights* in Arabia, which has as its frame story the plot of Scheherazade to ward off a death sentence. Both groups of stories bear witness to the inventive spirit of the storyteller and the storyteller's mission to transcend the constraints and pains of the natural order of things. Such tales are excellent sources for story ideas and provide a wealth of suggestions for initiating storytelling opportunities.

The long and troubled conquests of Wales and Ireland by England eventually broke down the famous storytelling schools; and the storytellers who might have traveled to them took, literally, to the open road. The thirteenth and fourteenth centuries were the romantic age of the itinerant bards and minstrels throughout Europe and the Near East. Thousands of men and women passed from town to town and country to country, telling stories as one of a number of entertainments, including juggling, acrobatics, and dramatic skits. As the bards and minstrels performed more and more often in public squares and marketplaces rather than in the courts and homes of the rich, their stock of tales gradually shifted from stories about kings, queens, and milestones of history to stories about common folk, familiar animals, and popular superstitions.

The freelance storytellers of the Middle Ages survived from day to day solely on their ability to command a listener's attention and transport that listener to a new world. Descendants of troubadours marked off their spaces next to the merchants at French fairs and sought to attract the notice of wealthy patrons with their stories of the hero Roland or Reynard, the crafty fox. Moslem *rawis* chanted the tales that were to become *The Thousand and One Nights* in

Baghdad street bazaars. *Skaziteli,* either obeying a religious vow of poverty or else blind and old and useless for other work, wandered from village to village in Russia weaving marvelous anecdotes to illustrate scraps of peasant wisdom. Ivan the Terrible employed three skaziteli to while away his hours of insomnia. In Germany, mastersingers competed with each other at public gatherings, a situation Wagner immortalized in *Die Meistersinger.*

New worlds of storytelling

In the fifteenth century, two events profoundly altered the nature of storytelling: the invention of the moveable-type printing press around 1440 and the European discovery of the Americas in the 1490s. Today the whole character of what we consider to be "a story" and of how we practice storytelling derives from the impact of these developments on the popular imagination of the Western Europeans who capitalized on them and quickly transformed themselves into citizens of the world.

Thousands of stories had been recorded during the preceding three thousand years since the Egyptian papyrus containing "The Tale of Two Brothers"; but before the advent of modern printing, the manufacture of a book was a time-consuming and very expensive process. A scribe typically invested five or six months of full-time labor to fill two hundred pages of sheepskin. Less costly books were fashioned by artisans who carved entire pages on single wooden blocks that were then handpressed on wood-pulp vellum; however, the quality of these books was usually mediocre and most of the content was pictorial.

Only a small fraction of the general population was literate—and of this fraction, very few could afford the purchase of more than one or two texts in a lifetime. Inevitably, the majority of texts committed to paper in the centuries following the birth of Christ were Latin or French, the two most prominent languages, and so the cultural products of societies who used other languages were poorly represented.

Gutenberg's wondrous new machine radically changed this picture in an astonishingly short time. The screw-and-lever press proved so versatile, reliable, and cost-effective that soon written treatments of thousands of subjects in dozens of different languages

Scheherazade

"One of my favorite stories in the world is 'Scheherazade,' the frame story of *The Thousand and One Nights*," says John Barth, the famous American novelist. "For a time, I regarded it as an insightful work of feminist fiction. Later in my own education as a writer, I came to regard the story as a metaphor for the condition of narrative artists in general."

A frame story is one that provides a context and excuse for a limitless series of independent "substories." In Irish tradition, the eleventh-century *Storyteller* cycle is framed by the tale of a storyteller who must repeatedly find a new story to compete in the king's festival or else face a serious calamity. The frame story of the eleventh-century Indo-Persian story cycle, *The Thousand and One Nights* is the story of Scheherazade. The number "1001" is not to be taken literally. "One thousand" in Arabic means "innumerable"; and it is for innumerable nights that Scheherazade is compelled to spin tales for her king.

After learning of the unfaithfulness of his wife and the wife of his brother, King Shahrayar joins his brother in vowing never again to give a woman a chance to betray him. Every night he demands his vizier bring him a virgin to share his bed. The next morning, she is killed. At last no virgins remain in the realm except the vizier's two daughters. His elder daughter, Scheherazade, insists on being presented to the king that night, overriding her father's strenuous protests by promising that she has a means of deliverance. She also insists that her sister, Dunayazade, attend her.

That night, as Scheherazade and the king prepare for bed, Dunayazade enters their chamber and begs Scheherazade, "Tell us some of your wonderful tales." The king consents and Scheherazade complies. When the morning comes, she has still not finished one of the tales; and the king, eager to hear the conclusion, postpones her execution until the next morning. And so it continues, for innumerable nights, until the king realizes that the storyteller is a person who can restore happiness and trust, and so he marries her—and convinces his brother to cease his cruelty and marry Dunayazade.

Among the tales Scheherazade tells her king are "Ali Baba and the Forty Thieves," "Aladdin and the Magic Lamp," and "Sinbad the Sailor." Each story

has its own beginning, middle, and end; and some characters, like Sinbad, appear in numerous separate tales. All the tales, however, tell of the marvels that exist in the world of Scheherazade and the other protagonists in the frame story; and each story reflects one or more of the themes present in the frame story—treachery, terrible vengeance, fabulous power, cunning, and rescue. The same relationship between frame story and substories exists in the British cycle of stories organized around King Arthur and the Knights of the Round Table, which is contemporary to *The*

Thousand and One Nights.

The Indo-Persian culture that gave rise to *The Thousand and One Nights* revered the curative powers of storytelling, and one can see the continuation of this reverence into the modern era. Even today in Hindu medicine, a person who is mentally ill is given a fairy tale, the contemplation of which will help that person overcome his or her emotional disturbance. In Muslim societies, it is still customary when visiting sick people to tell them stories of endurance and triumph, many of them adapted from models that are centuries old.

were available in print to a mass audience. Literacy rates soared, increasing numbers of artists, scholars, and storytellers turned themselves into authors, and the people at large were exposed to a flood of stories from new sources. Even stay-at-home, hard-working pragmatists could now become captivating storytellers, thanks to the proliferation of books that gave them both tales to tell and stylistic narrative devices to imitate.

Unfortunately, while much was gained for the art of storytelling, much was lost as well. Professional oral storytellers declined in number and variety as storytelling evolved at one extreme into a commonplace domestic activity and at another extreme into an institutionally sponsored and highly precious performance event.

Even more threatening to creative storytelling was the fact that people began to consider the printed version of a story as the "correct" version of that story. This attitude persists today, so that many people feel inhibited when it comes to spinning a tale from memory if they know the tale exists in print. I encountered a particularly widespread and harmful version of such an inhibition while discussing this book last year with a young mother at a day-care center. "I prefer reading 'Snow White' aloud because I'm just not as good a storyteller as the person who actually wrote the story," she lamented.

The mother's comment reveals a confusion dating back to the Gutenberg era over the difference between the author of a book and the "creator" of the material it contains; but, more significantly, it also reflects an underlying attitude about the printed word that is potentially damaging in regard to the free exercise of other vital modes of communication. When the printed word first appeared, it was endowed with the character of "truth," and in its very permanence seemed to transcend the importance of transitory speech. We can still easily overdo our respect for the printed word and forget that the spoken word is a completely different medium of expression—with its own "truth" and, consequently, its own vocabulary, syntax, content, and delivery demands.

The Gutenberg era gave birth to a new kind of tale—the literary tale—which is a story created by a writer for the specific purpose of being read. Writers of literary tales cannot avoid mining the same themes and subjects that storytellers have mined since the beginnings of language; and most tales of this kind are, in fact, adaptations of stories that existed within the oral tradition. What makes them unique in the realm of stories is their distinctively literary style. Crafted to sustain the interest and attention of a reader, as well as to achieve the compositional standards of enduring works of literature, these tales are especially attractive to adults, whose appreciation for language has been heavily influenced by prose models. Expert authors of literary tales include Hans Christian Andersen, Oscar Wilde, Carl Sandburg, Eleanor Farjeon, Howard Pyle, Padraic Colum, Laurence Housman, and, in more recent years, Natalie Babbitt, Henry Miller, Isaac Bashevis Singer, Barbara Picard, and Jane Yolen.

The Gutenberg era also fostered the collection and preservation of time-honored tales in entirely new constructions. Around 1530, an anonymous writer published tales that had been popular in France for centuries about a benevolent giant called Gargantua. One reader, François Rabelais, was impressed enough with the results to compose his own stories about the giant's son, whom he named Pantagruel. He later incorporated these stories with the Gargantua stories. His *Gargantua and Pantagruel* became a much-beloved classic that reached five volumes by the time of his death. In England in 1596, Edmund Spenser published his epic poem, *The Faerie Queen*, containing hundreds of allusions to familiar Celtic folk and hero stories. Miguel de Cervantes wove age-old courtly romances into his picaresque novel *Don Quixote*, first printed in Spain in 1605. Perhaps the single most potent publishing event in terms of present-day storytelling was the appearance in 1812 of Jacob and Wilhelm Grimm's *Kinder- und Hausmärchen*, an extensive collection of Germanic folklore that sparked an enormous interest in the study and perpetuation of traditional tales everywhere in the Western world.

During the same period of time that the printing press was working its revolution in humankind's capacity to communicate, the discovery and colonization of the Americas was working its revolution in humankind's capacity to imagine. A whole new world of experiences offered and demanded a whole new world of stories. Tall tales of the exotic flora and fauna abounded, beginning with Christopher Columbus' accounts of sirens leaping in the sea and one-eyed men with the faces of dogs. As waves of immigrants poured into the land that became the United States of America, a great melting pot of folklore was created. Settlers from the British Isles brought their "Jack" tales, such as "Jack and the Beanstalk," to

Appalachia, where they assumed fresh identities as they accumulated details from the daily lives of new American tellers. A similarly rich cycle of tales transported by African slaves eventually
took the shape of the "Br'er Rabbit" stories collected by Joel
Chandler Harris. Swedes and Spaniards, the Chinese and the
Dutch, Italians and Scots, Hungarians and Hawaiians exchanged
stories from their cultures and influenced each other and ultimately
produced distinctively American tales: tales of unprecedented wonders and miraculous lives. Van Wyck Brooks touched on this
phenomenon when he wrote about the western frontier around
1800:

> One heard of watermelons as large as houses and trees on the Miami
> River in which honey grew, springs of rum and brandy that gushed
> from the Kentucky Hills and flax-plants that bore woven cloth in
> their branches. With these humorous yarns were mingled others that
> might have been true; and how was a credulous Easterner to draw the
> line? Was there not really perhaps a hoop snake that spun through the
> swamps like a wheel, a whip snake that killed cattle with the lashing
> of its tail and a serpent that exhaled a fatal gas? These tall tales that
> crossed the mountains were true as intimations that almost anything
> indeed might happen in the West. The West possessed the largest
> rivers; and were not the storms more terrible there, were not the bears
> more dangerous than anywhere else? Moreover, the true frontiers-
> man, whom one sometimes saw in Philadelphia, striding through the
> streets with the step of an Achilles, suggested that he could manage
> the storms and the bears. No tales about the West could ever seem tall
> to anyone who saw him with a rifle. He could perforate a milk-pail
> half a mile away, he could enlarge the tin eye of the cock on the
> steeple, he could split a bullet on a razor at a hundred paces and cut
> the string of a flag at three hundred yards. This William Tell was a
> walking and visible legend.

But the land was full of stories ages before it became known as the
United States of America. In longhouses and ceremonial clearings
during the winter months of enforced leisure, when the potentially
dangerous spirit influences of summer were absent, native American
storytellers retold ancient legends about the creation of that land,
about the supernatural forces that tend it, and about the forms of
life that it supports. Many of these tribal wise people held special
status in their communities as moral and religious guides and

distinguished themselves by wearing long ropes of animal teeth or feathers that numbered their tales and served as mnemonic devices.

Some of the native American stories mirror characters, plots, and themes of stories that flourished independently in Europe, Asia, and Africa, confirming the notion that all stories share common roots. The personality and stratagems of Odysseus can be recognized in tales of the Huron hero Scianto. The foolish Cherokee hunters who think that the moon has drowned in a local lake and must be rescued have their counterparts in the Irish story of Hudden and Dudden. The footrace of the fox and the turtle recounted by the Onondagas is a close relative of Aesop's fable of the tortoise and the hare. Even such American-born freaks as the Yeti or Sasquatch—seven-foot-tall humanoid monsters in Pacific northwest Indian legends—find their kin in Tibetan tales of Abominable Snowmen.

Other native American stories, however, exhibit a unique closeness to nature that had a pronounced influence on the storytelling imaginations and listening tastes of generations of white settlers who came to inhabit the same territory. Among them are the haunting bird tales of the Navajos, the Sioux legends that envision the sun as a youth at dawn and a glowing red swan at dusk, and the Cheyenne myths about how the powers of earth, air, fire, and water gave substance to the Great Plains.

As an American, I am especially drawn to Indian tales. Stories about haunted castles, or crafty leprechauns, or genies trapped in oil lamps charmed me when I was a child; but I could not take them to heart. A great deal of their appeal lay in their exoticism; and children need to believe that the very land on which they live has a rich legacy of marvels. Indian stories I heard at summer camp and on travels through the western United States spoke of that land to me and gave me a privileged sense of inheritance.

I will end this discussion of stories and storytelling as I began it—with a story. It is a highly appropriate tale from the Seneca tradition, and one that is particularly appealing to a youngster who is fascinated by rocks, as I was:

THE STONE THAT TOLD STORIES

A long time ago in the forests of what was later called "New York," a young orphaned boy was hunting for food to bring home to his grandmother. Late in the afternoon, he was sitting on a large stone, making new points for his arrows when he heard a voice say, "I have a present to give you—a story." The boy looked all around him and could see no one. It could only be this stone that spoke, he thought; so he looked at the stone and said, "What did you say you would give me?" "A story," the stone answered. "But first you must give me a present."

The boy gave the stone one of the partridges he had caught, and the stone told him a story about the first people, who lived in the sky. It seems one of these people was an old woman who dreamed that a large tree in her village should be dug up by its roots. When the villagers heard her dream, they obeyed it and dug up the tree. But they were so angry about the hole it left in the sky that they turned on the old woman and threw her into it. She began falling toward earth, which was completely covered by water then. All the animals swimming in the water had to pull the earth up from the water, place it on the back of a turtle, and pat it dry so that it could receive her when she finished falling.

The boy thanked the rock for the story and promised to return the next day with another present so that he could hear another story. This went on for days, until at last his friends asked him, "Where do you disappear every afternoon?" The boy told them about the storytelling stone and brought them with him to hear it speak. Soon the whole tribe went every day to listen to the stories. For four years the stone told stories; and then one evening, after the other people had left, the stone said to the boy, "In years to come you will be old and unable to hunt and the stories I have told you will help you live. Tell them to others, but make sure they give you something in return. I have told you all the stories. Now it is time for people to keep the stories." And the stone became silent and never spoke again.

The boy grew up and grew old. He told his tales to people far and near and always received praise, or food, or love for the telling. That is the way stories came to be and why there are many stories in the world today when there were none before. We cannot stop telling stories about the people from the other world before us, the ones of whom the magic stone spoke.

Pathways To Storytelling

- Read several versions of the same story. It will give you some idea of just how flexible a basic story situation is and will inspire you to adapt stories you already know in many different ways. Numerous tales featuring Cinderella (a.k.a. Vasilisa, Nomi, Zezolla, and so on) are described in Marian R. Cox's *Cinderella: Three Hundred and Forty-Five Variants*. Padraic Colum's "The Girl Who Sat by the Ashes" and Eleanor Farjeon's "The Glass Slipper" represent beautiful literary versions of the tale. Rumpelstiltskin appears in different collections as Tom Tit Tot and Whipperty Stourie. Almost any story included in a Brothers Grimm anthology ("Sleeping Beauty," for example) exists in many other widely available forms. The tales of foreign storytellers, such as Hans Christian Andersen, are typically reprinted not only in many different translations but also in many different abridgements.

- Explore books about the history of storytelling, such as Ruth Sawyer's *The Way of the Storyteller* (which also includes a selection of her favorite tales), Anne Pellowski's *The World of Storytelling*, and Jane Wilson's *The Story Experience*. Bruno Bettelheim's book *The Uses of Enchantment* is a highly readable account of the impact of stories on children and offers excellent summaries of both familiar and unfamiliar tales. Also compelling are books in which the subject of storytelling plays a significant role. Among these are Alex Haley's *Roots*, Ian Yoors's *The Gypsies*, and any one of the popular series of *Foxfire* books.

- Attend a professional storytelling event at your local school, library, museum, or folklore society, or research storytelling opportunities that may present themselves while you are traveling, especially to areas that regularly conduct festivals. Make sure the storytelling consists of spoken stories rather than read-aloud stories. Secure a list of the stories to be told in advance or ask the teller for sources following the event. With the teller's permission, you may want to tape the stories.

- Think about the synopses of stories offered in this chapter. Practice adapting them, adding your own touches. Change the characters or environment or physical features of the stories. Think of equivalent stories or more contemporary examples of the same themes.

CHAPTER TWO

TYPES OF STORIES

How does one go about becoming a storyteller? Where does one begin? There is certainly no lack of material. Millions of stories that have already been proved capable of entertaining children lie waiting for us in books, and these represent only a fraction of the stories that continue to be passed along by word of mouth. We spend a major portion of our lives listening to many different varieties of stories—running the gamut from highly edited television news stories to the rambling anecdotes spun by our relatives, friends, and acquaintances. And even more to the point, there is ample evidence that we are all natural creators of stories. We can effortlessly weave fantasies for our own amusement or translate memories of past events in our lives into fresh and compelling narratives for each new person we meet. Even while we sleep, our minds give birth to stories in the form of dreams.

Dreaming, in fact, is the human activity most closely related in spirit to what I mean by "creative storytelling." Off and on during my life I have kept track of my dreams in special journals, and the notes I have made have inspired many successful children's stories. Two years ago I became one of three editors of the *Dream Network Bulletin*, a Brooklyn-based bimonthly newsletter linking thousands of professional and lay people in North America, Latin America,

Europe, the Soviet Union, the Philippines, Australia, and New Zealand who wish to share and discuss their individual and group dream-study experiences. As an editor, I have had the chance to study not only dreams that bear witness to an innate, universal storytelling capacity but also dreams that are directly concerned with storytelling itself. One dream in particular, recounted by a woman who is a children's librarian, has much to say about how one becomes a storyteller:

> I am standing on a white plain that stretches everywhere I look to an absolutely flat horizon. There are no features on the plain to distinguish it from the sky, which is bright but sunless. I want to move but can't decide which direction to go. Finally, I take a step to the left. Suddenly the landscape at my feet seems to reveal some detail, as if there were symbols or letters there. I take a few more steps and the whole landscape begins to come to life with different details in different places. I'm too excited to stop and try to make out what any of these symbols or words are saying. I feel exhilarated and begin to dance.

We can easily develop a kind of "hysterical blindness" when it comes to storytelling: one that prevents us from seeing any of the multitude of stories that surrounds us. All that we see is a vast blankness, at once frightening and hypnotizing, as the whiteness of Moby Dick is to Captain Ahab. This librarian's dream begins much like dreams that torment actors about being on stage with no idea of what they should say or dreams that I had occasionally during the years when I was a teacher about facing a class full of students and not knowing what topic I was supposed to cover.

Such dreams are, at the very least, intriguing starting points for stories; but they can also nudge us to become more aware of the nature of our capabilities. They are perhaps designed by our unconscious minds to tease our conscious selves into recognizing that the power to accomplish any feat rests within us. All we have to do is overcome our inertia. Once we do, we will know where to go whether or not there is a clearly visible goal by which to set a course. We will communicate whether or not there is a specific script to recite.

What is significant about the history of stories and storytelling is not necessarily that it has generated countless numbers of individual stories for us to exploit. Far more important is the fact that it has produced and refined a few basic, time-tested story models that all storytellers can use to give substance and structure to their own stories. Some of these self-created stories may indeed be informed by the tales they have already read or heard; but, like the dance of the librarian in her dream, each story proceeds according to a pattern they themselves have internalized and can employ again and again to tell as many stories as they wish.

All stories for children are stories about human experience; and they can be categorized into seven major types: formula tales, fables and parables, fairy tales, folktales, myths, legends, and realistic adventure stories. Understanding and distinguishing among these different types of stories will help you to take the first and most valuable step toward becoming a more effective storyteller. Before focusing on each individual type of story, however, consider for a moment what every good story for children has in common.

A child is vitally interested in news—the ever-shifting interplay of "who, what, when, where, why, and how." The most appealing stories are those that introduce unexpected or atypical twists into this arrangement: a mysterious "who," a strange "where," a novel "why." A story about a normal man building a normal house does not excite and challenge a child's creative imagination nearly as much as a story about a pig building a normal house or a normal man building a house in an underwater kingdom. It is fair game for the child to wonder about pigs performing human tasks or about underwater kingdoms. Somehow, it is not quite fair game to wonder about how a normal man builds a normal house. This is part of adult knowledge, which children have faith that they can acquire, should they need to or want to, sometime in the future.

Another fundamental characteristic of every good children's story is that the plot revolves around an element of tension. In some stories the tension is provided by an overt conflict, such as a battle between two characters or the struggle of a single character with his or her environment. In other stories, the tension is the contrast between two different situations or points of view or modes of behavior. A popular Chinese story, for example, explores the contrasting worlds of the silver creatures of the moon and the golden creatures of the sun who never fight with each other but who respond to each other by developing wondrously opposite lifestyles. In yet other stories, the tension resides simply in suspense. When will the shepherd be rescued? Will Bullethead come back? Where is the secret cache of rubies?

Any good children's story is an action-oriented story. The plot moves by one event leading immediately to another, with a minimum of descriptions, explanations, or asides. Devices that work well in adult literature, such as flashbacks, reflective monologues, or dialogues that convey attitudes, tend to interfere with the narrative momentum that compels attention in a children's story.

Finally, every well-turned children's story is essentially a puzzle that delights and sustains the imagination of the listener. Beyond the tale and its telling resides a meaning and a purpose, never to be too directly stated or the puzzle loses its mysterious allure. Perhaps a given story offers a symbolic examination of real-life hopes and fears. Perhaps it stimulates speculation about how things came to be or about cause-and-effect relationships. Perhaps it encodes advice about the value of different human experiences or about how to achieve different desired outcomes. Perhaps it works to restore the listener's sense of perspective or to provide the listener with contentment or ambition. Whatever caused the story to exist, the finished story acquires a symbolic force that transcends simple definition, even when the story itself contains a specific moral.

As you read about each separate story type, recall the characteristics common to every children's story and think about how each type applies these characteristics in a distinctive manner.

Formula Tales

Formula tales, in a strict sense, are not tales at all. They may be more accurately described as tales about tale-making. Their power resides not in plot content but in the playful exercise of narrative patterns. Their effect is to stimulate wonder and delight about the possibilities of language and the logical frameworks we give to our perceptions. Although they possess all the characteristics of a good children's story, they come closer to being games than any other type of story because they celebrate nonsense. Nevertheless, they display much wisdom and beauty, and they are always logical on their own terms.

The most common kind of formula tale is the "chain story," in which some series of characters, events, numbers, words, or response patterns is linked together in a formal relationship that is sustained throughout the story. A popular type of chain story is the one that extends a single occurrence to an absurd length: a yawning old man who swallows a fly, then swallows a spider to catch the fly, then swallows a bird to catch the spider, then swallows a cat to catch the bird, then swallows a dog to catch the cat, then swallows a goat to catch the dog, then dies (unless the teller wishes to go further).

Another variation of the chain story is the "good news/bad news" story—for instance, the story of Ike and Mike:

Ike and Mike were sitting in the park and Mike asked Ike, "What's new?"

Ike said, "Two men went up in an airplane this morning."

Mike said, "That's good."

Ike said, "No, that's bad. The motor conked out."

Mike said, "That's bad."

Ike said, "No, that's good. They had a parachute."

Mike said, "That's good."

Ike said, "No, that's bad. The parachute didn't open."

Mike said, "That's bad."

Ike said, "No, that's good. There was a haystack directly below them."

Mike said, "That's good."

Ike said, "No, that's bad. There was a pitchfork hidden in the haystack."

Mike said, "That's bad."

Ike said, "No, that's good. They missed the pitchfork."

Mike said, "That's good."

Ike said, "No, that's bad. They missed the haystack."

A more sophisticated kind of formula tale is the kind where the main character falls victim to his or her own overelaborate fantasy. This example comes from Laos:

THE BAG OF RICE

Once there was a man who was too lazy to get a job. Every day he would wander in the streets and beg for his food. One day, a wealthy merchant took pity on him and gave him a bag of rice. The lazy man took it home and poured the rice into a pot, which he put at the foot of his bed. "Now I can lie down for the rest of the day," he sighed, "and dream of how I will make my fortune with this rice.

"When the crop is bad and the price of rice is high," he began, "I will sell my rice and buy a cow and a bull. They will have calves, which I can sell to buy a pair of buffaloes. When the buffaloes have calves, I can sell them and with that money I'll marry a strong, healthy woman. Then we'll have a child; and when the child is large enough to sit alone, I'll take care of it and let my wife work in the fields. If she says, 'No, I won't go out and work in the field,' I'll kick her!"

With that, he struck out his foot and knocked over the pot at the foot of his bed. It broke and the rice spilled out and fell through the cracks in the floor. The neighbors' pigs rushed over and ate it, and the lazy man had nothing left but his broken pot.

Formula tales are particularly easy to invent, develop, and adapt. They also have a unique way of appealing to the listener's playfulness and, if desired, can be used as models for participatory games (see Chaper 5).

Fables and Parables

The terms *fable* and *parable* are virtually interchangeable. Both denote a short tale specifically designed to communicate a truth or lesson about life. In common usage, *fable* has come to be associated with a story that expresses a piece of practical wisdom and features fantastic events or characters, often animals behaving as people. *Parable*, which etymologically means "the word," connotes a more serious kind of tale: one that dramatizes a moral or religious principle and has a more realistic plot.

Many fables and parables directly state the message they convey—Aesop's fables being perhaps the most well-known examples in the Western world. Other fables and parables are less explicit and rely more on the resources of the listener to give them meaning. A good illustration of this latter kind is "The Parable of the Lost Son":

Once there was a rich man who had two sons. One day the younger son said to his father, "I want my share of your estate now, instead of waiting for you to die." The father agreed and gave his younger son the money he would have inherited.

The younger son took the money and traveled to a distant land, where he wasted it on parties and wine and women. When he had spent the last of it, a great famine came to the land and he began to starve. He took a job feeding pigs; and still he was so hungry that even the pods he was giving to the swine looked good to him. At last he came to his senses and said to himself, "At home, the hired men have food enough and here I am, dying of hunger! I will go home to my father and say, 'Father, I have sinned against both heaven and you and am no longer worthy of being called your son. Please take me on as a hired hand.' "

So he returned home to his father. While he was still a long distance away, his father saw him coming and was filled with pity and ran and embraced him. His son said, "Father, I have sinned against heaven and you and am not worthy of being called your son—" But his father said to his servants, "Quick! Bring the finest robe in the house and put it on him. And kill the calf we have in the fattening pen, for we must celebrate my son's homecoming with a feast!" So the party began.

Meanwhile, the older son, who had been in the fields working, returned home and heard the music and dancing. He asked a servant what was happening and the servant said, "Your brother is back and your father has killed the fatted calf and is celebrating."

The older brother was angry and wouldn't go in. His father came out and begged him to join the party, but he replied, "All these years I've worked for you and never once refused a single thing you told me to do; and in all that time, you never gave me even one young goat for a feast with my friends. Yet when this son of yours comes back after wasting all the money you gave him, you celebrate by killing the finest calf you have!"

"Look, dear son," the father said to him, "you and I are very close and everything I have is yours. But it is right to celebrate. For he is your brother; and he was dead and has come back to life! He was lost and is found!"

As both an older brother and a sometimes prodigal son, I was particularly impressed with this parable when I first heard it. The plot intrigued me, and I recognized that what the father does is a good thing to do. Nevertheless, it did seem to me at the time that the older brother's complaint had merit. I accepted the father's judgment (he is, after all, the master of his household); but I could not completely agree with it. I was old enough to hear and enjoy the parable but too young to unravel it.

It took years of pondering and roaming in distant lands before I could appreciate the parable's full beauty. On the most mundane level, I began to wonder, Would I really rather have had the younger brother's life, with all its pain, simply because he wound up with the money and the banquet and escaped those years of labor? On a higher level, I realized more and more the special quality of the celebration that the father ordains and why it merits the fattened calf: in honor of brotherhood, human need, and a miracle—not just because the younger brother did something right.

Had this been explained to me when I first heard it, I doubt if I would have understood it; and certainly I would have been robbed of the growth experience I underwent by coming to grips with the parable on my own. As it was, when I first heard it, I liked it and kept it; and that was enough. Such is the special magic of sharing parables with children.

Fables and parables are very powerful educational tools; but like all stories, their power lies in speaking for themselves. Explicating a story for a child, or calling attention to the relationship between a story and a child's life, violates the storytelling contract by intruding on the independence of the listener.

Fairy Tales

The term *fairie* is of Old English origin and refers to inhabitants of a special parallel world that overlaps with the real world. It is not a world of superior or inferior creatures, necessarily, but of human-like creatures whose existence is governed by different natural and social laws. It is what J. R. R. Tolkien calls a "Secondary World." Fairy tales are stories turning on the magic that occurs when citizens of this Secondary World enter ours, be they called "fairies," "elves," "genies," "imps," "sprites," "gnomes," "pixies," "brownies," or "leprechauns." The same magic also occurs, of course, when somehow or other human beings enter that Secondary World. Lewis Carroll refers to this eventuality in his preface to "Sylvie and Bruno":

> I have supposed a Human Being to be capable of various physical states, and varying degrees of consciousness, as follows:
> (a) the ordinary state, with no consciousness of the presence of Fairies;
> (b) the "eerie" state, in which, while conscious of actual surroundings, he is *also* conscious of the presence of Fairies;
> (c) a form of trance, in which, while *un*conscious of actual surroundings, and apparently asleep, he (i.e., his immaterial essence) migrates to other scenes, in the actual world, or in Fairyland, and is conscious of the presence of Fairies.

Perhaps the label "fairy tale" became attached to any story for children featuring supernatural events because such a large portion of the stories inherited by the English-speaking world is derived from stories about the Celtic fairies developed and spread by the ancient Irish and Welsh storytelling schools. Fairies are little ones whose world is overshadowed by the real world; as such, they have had a particular, even transcendent, appeal to children.

Irish *seanachai* (pronounced "SHAN-a-kee"), bearing the same title as the recounters of history in the ancient Irish school of ollamhs, continue to earn their living telling stories throughout the Republic of Ireland, particularly in Connemara and Donegal, where Gaelic is still spoken. Michael Jack, local historian on the Irish island of Inishbofin, keeps the tongue of Paddy John Halloran, the community's last full-time seanachai, preserved in a tin of Three Nuns tobacco. Here is one of Paddy John's stories, worth relating in full since it contains not only so much information about fairies but also so many of the elements of a good children's tale.

THE LAZIEST LASS IN IRELAND

Long ago there lived a poor widow. She had one daughter, Eileen, the prettiest and the laziest girl in the whole of Ireland. One morning the widow was leaving early to do some work for a neighbor, and she said to Eileen, "Today you'll be doing your share of the work. Make our noontime pudding. You'll be taking care, for if you burn it, the two of us will go hungry all day."

Eileen sighed and slowly built up the turf on the fire and hung a pot of water over it. Stirring in the meal, she lost herself in a daydream. It was all about a life with no work, living in a castle, married to a fine prince. Suddenly she stopped dreaming, because smoke was pouring from the pot and making her cry. She ran outside and saw her mother standing on the step. The widow smelled the burning pudding and, for the first time in her life, raised her hand against her daughter, yelling, "The time has come to beat the laziness out of you!"

Who should be riding by just at this moment but the King of Ireland's son, who shouted, " 'Tis a shameful thing to be beating the girl!" The widow, who only wanted to speak well of her child, stopped and said, " 'Tis sad entirely that I do, but she won't stop working no matter how much I try to get her to rest." " 'Tis wondrous indeed," replied the prince. "For a year and a day I have searched for the prettiest lass who can work the best in the land. So if it's all the same to you, I'll be asking your daughter to come to my mother's castle and marry me." Eileen joyfully consented to go with the prince. And so, tossing a purse of gold to the widow, the prince lifted Eileen onto his horse and away they rode.

When they reached the castle, the queen met them and examined

Eileen closely. "She is pretty, I grant you," the queen said to her son, "but she has not the look of a lass that can work. Let her sleep here the night and on the morrow we will give her a fair test of her work."

The next morning when Eileen awoke, the queen led her to a spinning wheel and stool. Pointing to a pile of flax, she said, "You'll be spinning that flax into fine linen thread the day," and left Eileen to her labor. Eileen sat down, and for the first time in her life the shame of her laziness came over her. She wept for fear she would lose the prince that day; but then she heard a tapping on the window.

Looking up, Eileen saw a wee woman dressed in green with a wee red bonnet on her head. Eileen opened the window and let her inside. "The sound of your weeping brought me here," the wee woman said. "Why are you sad?" Eileen said, "All my life I have been lazy and have let my mother work for me. Now because I cannot spin, I'll not be let marry the prince, and I love him very much." "If you will make me a promise and keep it," replied the wee woman, "I will spin the flax for you." Eileen cried, "I will make you any promise and keep it." So taking a wee spinning wheel from under her cape and putting her foot on the treadle, the wee woman spun flax all day, singing, "Laugh, laugh, fairies laugh, when this is done—I wish me at the wedding of the queen's own son." When she had spun all the flax into fine linen thread, she said, "Don't you be forgetting, Eileen," and vanished in a whiff of green smoke. That evening the queen came to see her work, and said, "I see you can spin. We'll be seeing can you weave on the morrow."

The next morning, the queen led Eileen to a loom and a bench and said, "Today you'll be winding the shuttle and making cloth; if every bobbin of thread is not empty when I return, you'll not be marrying my son." Eileen sat down and began to weep again, and soon she heard a tapping at the window. There stood another wee woman dressed in green with a wee red bonnet on her head. Eileen let her in and told her of her troubles. "If you will make me a promise and keep it," said the wee woman, "I will weave the cloth for you." Eileen agreed, and taking a wee bench and loom and shuttle from under her cape, the wee woman began to weave the cloth, singing, "Laugh, laugh, fairies laugh, when this is done—I wish me at the wedding of the queen's own son." When all the bobbins were empty and the room was full of cloth, the wee woman said, "Don't you be forgetting, Eileen," and vanished in a whiff of green smoke. When the queen came that evening, she said, "I see you can weave. We'll be seeing can you knit on the morrow."

The third morning, the queen led Eileen to a small room stacked with yarn and said, "Today you'll be knitting all this yarn, or back to your mother you go." After she left, Eileen once again broke into tears, and once again she heard a tapping at the window. A third wee woman dressed in green with a wee red bonnet on her head was there, and Eileen let her in and told her why she wept. "If you make me a promise and keep it," said the wee woman, "I will knit the yarn for you." Eileen agreed, and taking wee knitting needles from under her cape, the wee woman sat down to knit, singing, "Laugh, laugh, fairies laugh, when this is done—I wish me at the wedding of the queen's own son." When the room was full of knitted stockings, she said, "Don't you be forgetting, Eileen," and vanished in a whiff of green smoke. When the queen came that evening, she said, "In faith, you must be the best worker in all of Ireland, and you'll be marrying my son on the morrow."

The next day Eileen and the prince were married, and the great and the grand of Ireland came to the wedding feast. "Let the meal begin," said the queen when all the guests were there. But just as she spoke, a knocking sounded at the door. When it was opened, in walked a wee woman dressed in green with a wee red bonnet on her head. "I am a guest of the bride," she said. " 'Tis true," Eileen answered. The queen motioned the wee woman to a seat but couldn't resist asking, "However did you come by that one monstrous foot of yours?" The wee woman said, "I have been spinning for hundreds of years. 'Tis the long pressing of the foot to the treadle that has made it grow." The prince said, "If that is what comes from spinning, I will never let my bride spin again."

Then came another knocking, and again a wee woman dressed in green with a wee red bonnet on her head came into the room and said, "I am a guest of the bride." " 'Tis true," Eileen answered. The queen motioned the wee woman to a seat but couldn't resist asking, "However did you come by those monstrous long arms of yours?" The wee woman replied, "For hundreds of years I've been weaving. 'Tis the throwing of the shuttle back and forth that has made them grow longer." The prince cried out, "If that is what comes of it, I'll never let my bride weave again."

A third time a knock sounded. A third wee woman dressed in green with a wee red bonnet on her head walked into the room and said, "I am a guest of the bride." " 'Tis true," Eileen answered. The queen was no longer shy but demanded right away, "However did you come by that monstrous great nose?" The wee women replied, "For hundreds of years I have been knitting, and the needles have hit my nose so many times that it has grown longer and fatter and redder." The prince shrieked, "If that is what comes of knitting, I'll never let my bride knit again."

The queen looked hard at the prince and Eileen, and at last she said, "I'm thinking that a bride who has the blessing of the fairy people is better than one who can spin, weave, or knit." And so the prince and Eileen lived joyfully and playfully together all the days of their lives.

"The Laziest Lass in Ireland" reveals the fairies, or wee ones, as creatures much like human beings. They pursue the humblest of trades—spinning, weaving, knitting, tinkering, shoemaking—and yet their skill greatly exceeds that of their human counterparts. They are part monstrous and part angelic, like humans, only more so. Their dress and manner bear proud witness to a distinctive social order that more closely resembles one huge family than the polyglot human communities they visit. They are benevolent by nature and quickly summoned by human tears, prayers, and invocations of the heart; but, high-spirited by nature, they are occasionally mischievous and quick to wield vengeance for a broken promise, a slight, or an injustice. And for all their magical powers and mysterious immunity from the vicissitudes of human fate, they delight in being recognized and honored by human beings.

In the Western world, the fairy tale, more than any other type of story, has established standards for what constitutes a good children's story. It has predisposed storytellers to step aside from the real world and say, "What if?" and has helped them develop themes and narrative devices that have worked successfully to entertain and educate countless generations of listeners. Among the themes are hope transcending despair, self-awareness as an essential component of passing from one phase of human existence to another, and the role of the miraculous in forging human destiny. And among the narrative devices created to serve such themes are symbolic transformation, repetition, the unknown covenant, the multifaceted challenge, and what James Joyce calls the "epiphany," or moment of revelation.

In "The Laziest Lass in Ireland," events on a human scale soon reach an impasse: Eileen no longer can function as a member of her mother's household. Miraculously, the moment of ultimate rejection for Eileen is also the moment her dream is set in motion. The prince appears and a "transcendental" life seems possible for her; but first she must pass through a lonely trial period, imposed by a "transformational" mother figure, the queen.

During this period, Eileen, cut apart from normal existence, becomes fully aware both of her laziness and of her love for the prince. It is a painful self-discovery that calls into being her "wee helpers," who also exist in a world set apart from normal life. She must strike a bargain with these forces to survive—a bargain the precise nature of which is unknown to her when she agrees to it. The challenge she faces has three parts to it, which is significant for several reasons. It symbolizes that there is more than one aspect to any challenging life circumstance: Winning a battle does not necessarily mean winning the war. It also allows for the depiction of gradual change. The tasks Eileen faces are increasingly more sophisticated: first, the creation of thread, then of cloth, then of garments themselves.

Repetition in "The Laziest Lass in Ireland" occurs on different levels and satisfies different story purposes. The wee women are all dressed alike and exact the same promise, which creates a comforting rhythm in a story of bizarre events and also implies that the same coping mechanism must be repeatedly applied to be effective. The three separate entrances to the wedding feast mirror the three separate visits to Eileen in her isolation, lending the story structure a pleasing parallelism, a sort of plot-rhyming. The continual repetition also serves to fix events in the mind of the listener and to make the story easier to recall. The "epiphany" occurs when all the characters are together and Eileen's essential self is vindicated.

You can find many of these same elements and devices in other stories—for example, in "Spider and the Box of Stories"—but in no other type are they more neatly and effectively embodied than in the true fairy tale. As a creative storyteller, you need only paint some character into a corner and then say, "All at once there was a tapping at the window," and off you can go!

Folktales

Folktales are stories that mirror human behavior, albeit in a fanciful way. They are similar in structure to fairy tales but more firmly rooted within a particular earthbound society; and so they yield special insights into the nature of the human condition: its joys and sorrows, opportunities and constraints, methods and madnesses, manners and mores.

Typically, an individual folktale preserves much of the flavor of the particular land and people from which it came; but folktales as a genre imaginatively portray universal human longings—the desire to hold communion with other living things; the dream of realizing fame, fortune, and love; the wish to master fate and the forces of nature; the yearning for justice, beauty, truth, and liberty. In folktales, men and women may be symbolized by animals, the landscape they populate may be phantasmic, and the events that unfold may assume superrealistic proportions; nonetheless, they merge in a logical fashion to communicate some aspect of what it is like to live in the real world.

Every now and then I am awakened in the predawn hours by the hooting of an owl that makes its home, improbably, in a block-long jungle of backyard trees only a few hundred feet from the borough hall of Brooklyn. It never fails to remind me of one of the most beautiful folktales I know. I first heard it at a Central Park storytelling hour conducted by Diane Wolkstein, who collected it during one of her pilgrimages to Haiti, where oral storytelling continues to thrive. I had a cold, Diane Wolkstein (I later learned) had back trouble, and the weather was turning increasingly blustery; but the tale cast a spell of wonder and enchantment over everyone who experienced it. It is entitled, simply, "Owl" and serves as an outstanding illustration of what a folktale is all about. I merely summarize the folktale here; Diane Wolkstein has recorded it in full, as it was originally told to her, in her fascinating book, *The Magic Orange Tree.*

Owl thought that he was very ugly, and that no one could ever love him. But one night he met a girl who talked with him and seemed to like him. "If the sun had been shining and she had seen my face," Owl said to himself, "she never would have liked me."

Every evening Owl went to visit the girl and they would sit on her porch and talk. They grew fonder and fonder of each other, until finally the girl's mother asked her, "Why doesn't Owl ever visit you during the daytime?" The girl answered, "Owl says he is busy working then and is only free to see me after the sun sets." "Well," said the mother, "I'd like to get a good look at him before you marry. Let's invite him to come over and dance on Sunday afternoon."

The girl invited Owl the next time he came over, and he was thrilled. "Just think," Owl said to himself, "a party in my honor!" But Owl was also scared to show his face, so he went to his cousin Rooster and asked him to go with him. As they rode their horses to the girl's house on Sunday, Owl noticed how handsome Rooster looked and how elegantly he was dressed and became very sad. "I can't go on," Owl said at last. "You go and tell them I've had an accident and will come later." Rooster agreed and rode on.

Owl waited until the sun had set and, finally, sneaked up to the girl's house and signaled Rooster to come to him. When Rooster came, he said, "Owl, whatever are you wearing on your head, I mean, your face?" Owl said, "It's a hat. Haven't you ever seen a hat before? Tell them I've scratched my eyes on a branch and the light hurts them. And you must be careful to watch for the sunrise and to crow as soon as you see it so we can get away." Rooster agreed and led Owl back to the house, where he introduced Owl to all the girl's relatives.

At first, Owl was shy and tried to hide himself, but the girl came over to him, smiled, and said, "Come into the yard and dance with me." Owl loved to dance and so he danced and danced and danced and lost all track of time. Suddenly, he heard Rooster crowing, but it was too late. The girl's mother came over and lifted Owl's hat, so that she and her daughter could finally see his face. "MY EYES!" Owl cried and, shielding his face with his hands, ran to his horse. "Wait please, Owl!" the girl called. And as Owl put his hands down to untie his horse, she saw his face. It was striking and proud, and the girl thought it was the noblest face she had ever seen in her life. But Owl was already gone, riding farther and farther away on his horse.

Owl never returned. The girl waited for him, but at last she gave up and married Rooster. She led a happy life, except for some mornings when she heard Rooster crow and wondered what had happened to Owl and where he was.

Myths

Ambrose Bierce, the American humorist, said it best in his dictionary:

> *Mythology*, n. The body of a primitive people's beliefs concerning its origins, early history, heroes, deities and so forth, as distinguished from the true accounts which it invents later.

Myths are stories that dynamically embody the religious or philosophical beliefs of a particular culture. Myths portray the actions of gods or godlike beings—detailing their attributes and rituals as well as their relationships to one another, to humans, and to the existence of natural phenomena. A myth is not a mechanism of amusement, which can become outdated or irrelevant; rather it is

The Trickster

One of the most beloved figures appearing in all types of stories from virtually every culture in human history is the trickster. Alternately clever and foolish, heroic and villainous, the trickster represents the best and the worst in all of us.

Often the trickster is represented as part human, part animal, and part divine—a character whose physical appetites dominate his or her behavior and who exercises magical cunning in gratifying those appetites. The trickster, in short, is not unlike a child. Through stories about the trickster, we learn to accept the inconsistencies and ambivalences in ourselves and others.

Among the North American Plains Indians, the most common trickster is the coyote, who once hurled fire into the sky so he could spy on the other creatures at night, thus creating the stars. Among the woodland tribes of the East, the main trickster is the Great Hare. Slaves from Africa combined tales of the Great Hare with their own legends of the trickster rabbit to form the well-known Br'er Rabbit cycle of stories.

European culture has produced numerous tricksters for different types of tales. From Reynard the Fox to Puss-in-Boots to Jack the Giant-killer to Prometheus, the European trickster is a character with a gambler's instinct, whose activities can result in either benefit or harm to other individuals or to humans in general.

An especially fascinating European trickster is the character in Scandinavian mythology called Loki, variously described as a giant, a god, a jester, and a demon. Loki, like the Greek Prometheus and the native American Raven, steals fire from heaven and brings it to earth—where it wreaks both good and evil. He is a companion to the great gods, Thor and Odin, diverting them with his antics, but he can also be their antagonist.

In one of the less cosmic and more typical tales, Loki wagers his head that Thor's smith cannot fashion a treasure more wondrous than the artificial gold hair of Sif, Thor's wife, which Loki himself commissioned two dwarfs to create after he prankishly cut off all of Sif's real hair. One day he sees the smith working on a hammer for Thor: a wonderfully powerful instrument that will cause thunder on earth whenever Thor

uses it to fight the evil forces of chaos and destruction. Fearing that he may lose his wager, Loki turns himself into a fly and bites the smith's eyelid just when the smith is cutting the handle. Although the handle is too short, the hammer is judged the most wondrous treasure after all by the assembly of the gods. Loki manages to keep his head, insisting that his neck was not included in the wager; but the gods sew his lips together so he will not be able to use his mouth to trick others.

The trickster figure in children's tales is a special breed of underdog, pitting his or her cunning and inferiority against an adversary's strength and stupidity. Whether the trickster is a maverick semideity, an alley cat, an abused servant girl, a sorcerer's apprentice, or a Tom Thumb, the trickster operates by his or her wits, exploring and exploiting the possibilities each different moment of life presents.

an ever-vital mode of perception by which the human mind can make order out of chaos and sense out of the manifold mysteries existing in life. Myths are poetic alternatives to scientific accounts of how the universe was created, of how men and women came to be and why they behave the way they do, of how natural forces operate, and of how social, political, and sacred customs developed. Both myth and science are human inventions and both have the object of inspiring study, understanding, reverence, and responsible action.

The ancient Greek and Roman myths, the Viking myths, and even the more obscure myths of the subjugated Celts and Anglo-Saxons long ago found their way into print. Today they are often taught in the classroom, enabling children and those who would exercise their childlike imaginations to learn more about the qualities of faith and wisdom that helped shape Western civilization. Only in very recent times, however, have the myths of native Americans been assembled and retold among the disparate peoples who have inherited the spectacularly well conserved and bountiful land that these myths describe. A Haida Indian myth about the origin of light perfectly conveys the simplicity, playfulness, and regard for nature that is pervasive in native American mythology.

RAVEN AND THE BALL OF DAYLIGHT

In a time when the world was still covered with darkness, Raven flew close to the surface and felt sorry for the men straining their eyes to hunt for food and the women straining their eyes to make shelters and clothing. He set off to the Chief of the Sky, who kept the Ball of Daylight safely hidden among his treasures. To get into the house of the Chief of the Sky, Raven turned himself into a spruce needle that fell into a spring and was swallowed by the Chief's daughter, who came to drink.

Soon the Chief's daughter became pregnant and gave birth to a son, who was Raven in disguise. The Chief was very pleased with the child, and eventually he allowed the child the special privilege of handling the Ball of Daylight. One day, the child rolled the Ball of Daylight to the door and, turning himself back into Raven, flew from the Chief's house with the Ball of Daylight on his back. When Raven reached the world of humans, he broke open the ball and set it rolling, so that the bright light would help the men to hunt and the women to make shelters and clothing.

Legends

Legends are stories about people, places, or events that have some basis in historical fact. Such stories often embroider details, or endow them with exaggerated and magical qualities, so that they become articles of popular belief rather than verifiable truths. Tales about Robin Hood, Lady Godiva, Davy Crockett, the headless horseman, Johnny Appleseed, John Henry, Pocahontas, and George Washington may fall into this category; so may stories about Christmas, a local haunted house, lover's leap, or robber's nest; the Loch Ness monster, the Chicago fire, and the Seven Cities of Cibbola.

Among the legends I most loved hearing as a child were the legends surrounding Paul Bunyan, his foreman Johnny Inkslinger, and his cook Sourdough Sam (a.k.a. Hezekiah Saltpeter). In retrospect, I realize that these legends crystallized for me the great spirit of the American pioneer I was asked to emulate in my own coming-of-age. They also offered me a conceptual framework by which I could contemplate the grandeur of the American landscape and the enormous human energy that had tamed it.

Paul Bunyan dug the St. Lawrence River, the Mississippi River, and Puget Sound, built the Rocky Mountains, carved the Grand Canyon, and cleared the Great Plains. His shovel became Florida and his mitten, Michigan. The Black Hills are the earth he piled on top of the grave of Babe, his beloved Blue Ox. Although I always had the sense that there was a real man behind the legend—or a whole community of men—it was not until I grew up and did some research that I discovered the legends derived from the adventures of a French Canadian hero, Jean-Paul Bonhomme, a key figure in the Papineau Rebellion of 1837 against the effete colonial administrators of Queen Victoria's government.

Legends are uniquely effective in communicating to young listeners the metaphorical significance that particular human beings, places, and events accumulate within a given cultural context. Children know that history suggests meanings and messages that are far greater in scope than the facts themselves can reveal, and they welcome and appreciate the symbolic rendering of history represented in legends as an off-the-record means of indulging this knowledge.

Realistic Adventures

"Realistic adventure" is a catch phrase I use to describe the most common type of story—a less formal type than the ones we usually associate with storytelling. A real-life adventure is any narrative of something that actually happened or could actually happen, which, by virtue of being an adventure, satisfies the basic characteristics of a good story: It is "news," it presents tension in the form of conflict or contrasting elements, it is action-oriented, and it has a purpose.

A real-life adventure can be about something that happened to you or a member of your family. It can be based on a biographical sketch of someone else. It can revolve around a sporting event or a historical incident or a spectacle of nature. It can be either fact or fiction, as long as the fiction reflects character types and life possibilities actually prevailing in the world as we know it. It is the type of story that emerges naturally in the course of a conversation or is most frequently featured in newspapers, magazines, books, films, and TV programs portraying interesting human situations. Realistic adventure stories that take place in an unusual locale or record exceptionally heroic deeds are exciting to any listener, and children are no exception. But children don't need to be over-powered by the exotic to be fascinated. There is enough stuff in everyday life to intrigue them.

Children particularly enjoy stories that tell them something about the teller. Such stories create an even stronger bond between the listener and teller than the act of storytelling itself, and the teller is apt to be more skillful and comfortable in presenting them since they are based on his or her own experience. You can develop a story around how your ancestors came to the United States, around the strange events that occurred after your car broke down in the Painted Desert, or around the first fight you had when you were a child.

Children also like stories involving people much like themselves. You can tell them stories drawn from what you know about the lifestyles of children in other families or other countries or other times. You can make up stories about children closely resembling your listeners who are trapped overnight in a department store or who run away to join the circus.

The Smithsonian Institution has been collecting stories of this variety for years, since they preserve narrative structures and subjects that are distinctively American. One of the most delightful tales was contributed by Pam Matlock, a native of Philadelphia, for the book *A Celebration of American Family Folklore.* It is, in a sense, a story within a story:

THE SANDBOX

My father used to make up Mit and Mat stories; I was Mat and my brother was Mit. The one I remember best is the one my brother doesn't figure in at all. We used to go to the beach every day; it was a very short drive from Philadelphia. We had a sandbox in the backyard and I was trying to get sand for it. My father used to bring a few buckets of sand back from the beach.

Well, Mat goes to the beach with her parents and she wants to bring sand back and her father says, "No, it won't fit in the car." So while they're sleeping on the beach, Mat fills the trunk of the car up with sand and then covers it over with towels. They drive home and Mat's father is very upset because the car isn't riding properly. He can't understand it. He says, "I'll have to take it to the garage and have them check it out." But as they get close to the Benjamin Franklin Bridge, the load becomes less; and the car is all right when they get home.

Well, Mat can't wait to get out and look in the trunk for the sand. But it is gone! It has come out in dribbles. She notices little dabs of sand in the driveway and she starts following it with her bucket, scooping it up. She ends up all the way back at the beach, at which point her parents are very upset and they call the police and there is a big search for this lost little girl. But they are glad to get her back home.

The upshot is that everybody reads about this poor little girl who doesn't have any sand in her sandbox. And they start sending sand. She gets sand from Arabia, sand from North Africa, and sand from everywhere, all over the world, all different colors of sand. The yard is full of it. It becomes ridiculous. There is too much sand. So she gets this wonderful idea. She makes the sand into bricks, beautifully colored bricks, different layers, and sells them for a quarter a piece. Pretty soon, she is back to having no sand in her sandbox and stealing it from the beach.

Your Type of Story

The seven basic story types outlined in this chapter were not consciously designed once upon a time by storytelling experts as models all professional and amateur storytellers must follow in order to be successful. They evolved naturally and logically as people began to communicate with each other for the purposes of educating and entertaining.

If there is one big trick to becoming a good storyteller, it is to make yourself aware of the forms that spoken stories usually take anyway, regardless of whether they are planned or not. Then you can allow your own instincts and inventions full rein and begin yarnspinning with full confidence that a story will result. And you can start making intelligent choices about what kind of story to tell on a given storytelling occasion.

Pathways To Storytelling

● In addition to reading different types of stories for children, try reading some literary tales written originally for an adult audience. The short stories of Isak Dinesen, Franz Kafka, Isaac Bashevis Singer, Nathaniel Hawthorne, and Edgar Allan Poe, among others, employ many of the best characteristics of a good children's story to serve highly sophisticated, adult-world themes. You may also want to listen to stories for an adult audience. Try tuning in Garrison Keillor, the creator and star of *A Prairie Home Companion*, which is beamed via satellite by American Public Radio to over two hundred radio stations every Saturday afternoon.

● Fables and parables are usually short and epigrammatic. They are fun to collect and compare and can easily be worked into conversations, letters, reports, and essays as well as into storytelling sessions. Investigate various collections of fables and parables, especially ones that reflect different cultural and religious modes of thought. Among the most popular fabulists are Aesop, Jesus, Buddha, Chaucer, Krylov, La Fontaine, and La Rochefoucauld.

● In most libraries and bookstores you will find many children's books devoted to the fairy tales, folktales, myths and/or legends of a specific region of the world. Usually this region is stated directly in the title: *Legends of the Eskimo, Hispanic Folk Tales, Myths of the Pacific, Stories from Appalachia*, and so on. Look through the books of several different regions and compare and contrast the stories you find.

● Pressed for a quick definition, I would describe a storyteller as one who delights in symbols—who enjoys finding them, living with them in his or her mind, and spinning narratives to communicate to others what they represent. Think of the following abstractions and the specific sensations, places, people, and objects that you associate with them: freedom, love, February, brother and sister, achievement. Using one or more of the symbolic images you develop, create your own formula story. Use the same image to create a fable or parable, a fairy tale, a folktale, a myth, a legend, and a realistic adventure story.

CHAPTER THREE

FINDING STORIES FOR DIFFERENT LISTENERS

Fables and parables, formula, fairy, and folktales, myths and legends, and realistic adventure stories did not originate specifically for telling to children. J. R. R. Tolkien, author of *The Hobbit* and *The Lord of the Rings*, reminds us in his essay "Tree and Leaf" that they became the property of children only by historical accident. As the human race developed more and more sophisticated social, political, professional, and informational systems, adult men and women necessarily became more and more preoccupied with nonfiction, "hard-copy" data oriented towards practicality. Less and less time was spent listening to stories. Instead, they read newspapers reporting current events, histories derived from empirical study, guidebooks documenting actual human experience, and philosophical works based on the exercise of rational thought.

The invention of printing, which increased the literacy rate among the population of Europe and made knowledge easier to acquire, and the Age of Exploration, which stimulated private enterprise and spread wealth and power among a broader base of people, combined in the fifteenth century to inaugurate a new phase of human intelligence. A steadily growing number of individuals began participating in "higher" education, and science came to overshadow imagination as the vehicle for investigating and articulating truths about the past, the present, and the future; the human being and society; the earthly realm and the universe.

What are now considered "children's stories" serve the vital function of offering mental stimulation and "truths" to those who are not yet intellectually prepared or psychologically predisposed to benefit fully from exposure to higher education. These stories are not a substitute for more "serious," or scientific, works. They are, rather, necessary precursors to understanding and appreciating these works, much as they were for the human race in general.

The childhood of each individual recapitulates the childhood of humankind. Children, like our ancestors, have a need to find their own answers to questions, their own solutions to problems, and their own ways of envisioning what they feel and perceive to be true. Constitutionally lacking the ability to satisfy these needs rationally, children inevitably turn toward fantasy. It is a fact of life to be exploited rather than denied. Through storytelling, adults can help children to cultivate their fantasies, so they can work through them and mature into adults capable of using their rational faculties effectively and creatively.

Just as the human race has undergone successive stages of intellectual development during its history, so do children pass through successive stages of intellectual development during the years between birth and the age of twelve, by which time most individuals have begun to experience the social and physical changes associated with sexual maturity. Different stories appeal to a child depending on his or her age group and, therefore, his or her probable developmental stage.

Before focusing on the general likes, dislikes, concerns, and characteristics commonly exhibited by children at different ages, however, there are several fundamental and overriding principles to consider when you are in the process of deciding what stories to tell a specific listener. The most important question to ask yourself at such a time is, What stories appeal to me, at this particular moment?

You stand the best chance of enjoying a storytelling session, and of communicating that enjoyment to your listener, if you are telling a story that you particularly like: not only one that is comfortable to you and charged with a certain amount of personal significance, but also one that matches your present mood. The story that first occurs to you may, indeed, be an instinctively correct choice for the occasion. In addition, a story you initially consider is likely to be one that is very familiar to you, and so it will be easier to adapt to a specific listener, especially if you have relatively little chance to get to know the listener, or the listener's frame of mind that day, before the storytelling session begins.

If you are uncertain about what story you want to tell, thinking about a child's actual or possible interests is bound to help you make an appropriate selection. Nevertheless, it is almost impossible to guess what will ultimately impress a child about a given story. A child possesses a much wider-ranging capacity to wonder than an adult does and is far more likely to involve himself or herself with the spirit and details of a story than an adult is. For these reasons, it is not accurate to infer that a particular story will only appeal to a particular kind of listener.

The same story offered to a child at different stages of his or her mental and emotional growth can continue to captivate his or her imagination in a different way each time it is told. For example, children exposed to Andersen's "The Steadfast Tin Soldier" at the age of four may be primarily intrigued by the physical setup of the playroom itself. They may associate the activity of arranging the soldiers on a table with their private delight in manipulating their own toys. They may also be fascinated by the mystical life of the soldiers, nutcrackers, and dolls after the people of the house have gone to bed—a mystical life they suspect their own toys of having and that roughly corresponds to their own bizarre dream existence while they are asleep. Seven-year-old children may be more engaged by the awesome adventures of the one-legged tin soldier away from the security of the playroom: his thrilling ride down the gutter, his dramatic encounter with the rat, his strange sojourn in the belly of the fish. Children who are nine or ten years old may be more inclined to identify with the one-legged tin soldier's personality and to respect his virtues of courage, constancy, and modesty. They may also savor the heroic and bittersweet quality of his love for the paper ballerina.

Ascertaining what a child enjoys about a particular story is a problematic task. It is best to avoid any direct inquiry, not only because it puts the child on the defensive but also because most children, like many adults, are unable or unwilling to articulate what really moves them on an intimate level. Children must protect themselves. They are understandably secretive among adults about their innermost feelings. Most children easily volunteer information about what they do not like, or what scares them; and this works as a dependable and invaluable aid in selecting a story or adapting it midstream in the telling. But children are much more shy and self-conscious when it comes to communicating what has pleased them. Frequently they will simulate what they think is the response you want to hear—and the patness of such a simulation can be disappointing and demotivating to the teller.

Try not to formulate concrete expectations concerning how your story will be received. Years of storytelling—or teaching, for that matter—have shown me that the individual who appears to be the most unresponsive may, in fact, be the one who has been the most impressed with what he or she has heard. Your listener's lack of comment or blankness of face may well be a natural consequence of his or her absorption in what you have said.

It is very unusual for children to rave about a story they have just been told. The whole atmosphere of the storytelling session makes this a blessedly unnecessary response. If a child does not appear to like a story, it may be for other reasons than the story itself. The child may be unalterably preoccupied with some deeper concern, and involuntarily expressing that preoccupation, but at the same time enjoying the contact and diversion provided by the storytelling session.

It is always wise to ask children if they would like to hear a story (any story—no one particular story) before launching into a storytelling session. Such a request simultaneously honors their independence and invites their cooperation and listening commitment. It is also enormously helpful to ask a child before you begin to tell a story what kind of story he or she would like to hear, providing you have a sufficiently broad repertoire of stories from which to choose. Just be sure that you address the child with open-ended questions when you are probing for story ideas. Asking a child if he or she would like to hear a story about a dragon can elicit an immediate no that casts a negative spell on the storytelling session.

Without a doubt, the best way to develop your ability to choose appropriate tales for different listeners is to enhance your observations of individual children and of the world of children in general. If you are around children on a consistent basis, take special note of their games; their personal habits; their prized objects; their interactions with peers, animals, and adults; their vocabulary; their daily patterns and mood cycles; their verbal and nonverbal responses to different events and challenges; the types of questions they pose; and the fears and hopes they reveal.

Pay particular attention to the television programs children watch, since television has such a large and potent influence on their mental development. According to the United States Department of Education, the average kindergarten graduate has already seen over 5,000 hours of television: more time than is required to obtain a bachelor's degree. If you are a parent concerned about getting to know your child better, you may want to establish a custom of regularly watching a particular children's television program together. This will not only give you a common source for certain story ideas, it will also condition both of you to fall more easily into the circumstances of a storytelling session, which is essentially a shared listening experience.

If you are not consistently around children, you can still make an effort to observe those whom you do encounter more closely. You, too, can experiment with watching television programming for children, reading books and articles about children, and imaginatively putting yourself in the position of a child. Recall your own childhood, the children you have known in your lifetime, and the images of childhood imparted to you by friends and relatives. Solicit impressions and insights from parents and from those who knew you when you were a child. Try to conceive what a furnished room or a neighborhood street or a store looks like to someone who is only two or three feet tall, or how a child might explain lightning, illness, the workings of a phonograph or tape deck, the rules and regulations of the adult world.

The commentary offered in this chapter for each age-group division represents a synthesis of my own observations; the testimony of parents, teachers, storytellers, and child-care professionals; and the published statements of major authorities on childhood. It is intended to provide you with a broad-stroke background of information to draw upon in determining your own storytelling choices. It won't equip you to become an amateur child psychologist, and your goal in choosing a story isn't necessarily to effect a correspondence between the story and a single aspect of a child's life. Sometimes this can be wonderful, but it can also backfire.

If you surmise, for instance, that a child repeatedly complains about an event that is not happening in order to receive attention, you may be tempted to tell that child the familiar story of the boy who cried "Wolf!" It may help the child to amend his or her behavior; but it may, on the other hand, make the child self-conscious and embarrassed. A safer choice would be to tell the child the story of Pinocchio, which discusses lying but also contains a wealth of other material for the child to ponder and does not confront a very sensitive issue so directly. The important part of your original observation is that the child seeks attention, and telling any story that appears to have been specially selected for his or her ears will be giving the child the attention he or she needs.

We may not know what story a child wants to hear, but we do know why the child wants to hear a story. Children are confined to rather narrow limits, in terms of their physical territory, their range of experience, their social status, and their rational ability to make sense of their environment. Stories open up passages for children to realms beyond these inhibiting boundaries. Bear in mind when you are choosing stories for an individual child that it is far better to overestimate his or her capacity to appreciate a story than it is to underestimate that capacity. The goals that make one stretch to reach them are the only goals that enable one to make progress—and the goals that one recalls with the most affection.

Birth to Five Years Old

You may be asking yourself at this very moment, "Why begin this category with 'birth'? What is the point of telling stories to new-born children? Just how much can they comprehend?" Typically, an infant does not seem to recognize voices and objects until the ninth or tenth month and begins speaking only after fifteen months. What good is storytelling during this first self-absorbed year and a quarter?

The answer is that storytelling, more than a transmission of characters, plots, and themes, is a unique form of communion between two people. What is valuable in the early years of storytelling is for the child to become accustomed to an adult's voice, especially a parent's voice, and to associate it with a peaceful time of day.

The infant who listens to any storyteller learns to enjoy on a precognitive level the particular rhythmic cadence that distinguishes a well-spun narrative from everyday chatter. Without any conscious effort on your part, your vocal delivery during storytelling is apt to be more musical, relaxed, and expressive than at other times; and your listener will remember these qualities later in life. Plus there is a delightful bonus for you as the storyteller in such a situation: You can tell any story you wish. You can rehearse stories without worrying about their logic, language, or structure.

Until your listener is a year and a half old, story content is essentially irrelevant. The act itself is all-important. The objective is not to work toward getting the child to understand your story, although individual concrete words like "daddy," "mommy," "dog," and "blanket" can be imprinted to provoke early comprehension. The objective is to condition the child to listen with open ears and to experience different sounds and tonal characteristics of speech.

Between the ages of a year and half and two years, children start speaking on their own—evidence that they have, in fact, been building a vocabulary over the preceding months. By the age of two, the average child can speak around 300 words and probably has a working knowledge of twice that many words. When a listener has begun to speak, you can begin to form very simple stories that enlist the child's understanding and encourage the child's efforts to become more involved in language.

From two to three years old, every child is a little Adam, fiercely bent on labeling everything his or her senses perceive in the immediate environment. Stories that name objects, define their function, and associate them with other objects are the most appropriate ones. At this stage of storytelling, you can easily create your own material. You'll do better to provide what are essentially chantlike word meditations rather than formal plot structures.

You can frame such a story by concentrating your attention on a single locale or a single group of items. For example, you may say, "In this room there is a ball, and the ball goes bounce, bounce, bounce. Mommy likes the ball and baby likes the ball and the ball is red and, whoops, the ball rolls away. In this room there also is a door . . ." and so forth. You can make stories of this type more dramatic by orchestrating a continuous flow of bodily movements and gestures to accompany what you are saying. In reference to the example I have just given, it is not necessary for you to handle the ball itself; in fact, this can be distracting. But the physical activity of first pointing to the ball and/or imitating its round shape with your hands, then pretending to bounce the ball, then hugging the imaginary ball to your breast, and finally pantomiming dropping the ball leads your listener to put together what you are saying conceptually, which supplements and extends his or her experiential understanding.

If storytelling gestures can evolve into a hand game, all the better. While still maintaining eye contact and spinning a "who, what, where, when, why, and how" story, you can boost a very young listener's ability to comprehend what you are saying by enlisting his or her fundamental modes of perception at this developmental stage—the senses of sight and touch. Take this story as a model:

> What does Daddy do when he gets up in the morning? He stretches and yawns (both stretch and yawn), he scratches his head (both scratch own head or each other's head), he puts on his clothes (both mimic dressing), he brushes his teeth (both mimic brushing own teeth or each other's teeth), he drinks his juice (both mimic drinking juice), he reads his newspaper (both mimic unfolding and reading a newspaper), he puts on his hat (both mimic putting a hat on own head or each other's head), he goes off to work (both wave at each other), he works all day long (both mimic an activity representing Father's work), and then he comes home (both wave at each other).

This particular story caters to the young child's interest in "what happens next?" and also serves a vital psychological function. Children of this age are liable to think, consciously or subconsciously, that when Mother and Father are not in view, they have disappeared and may not come back. This basic insecurity accounts for the popularity of simple "lost and found" or "now you see me, now you don't" stories. Rhythm, repetition, and humor—especially surprises, funny faces, and clever cross-references (like using your fingers to represent someone walking)—are particularly effective story ingredients for children up to three years old.

From two to five years old, a child is not only accumulating new words at an incredibly rapid rate, he or she is also mastering syntax. By the age of four, the average child has a speaking vocabulary of 1,600 words (the average adult, by comparison, uses only 1,800 words in routine daily life); and by five years of age, he or she is able to speak up to 2,100 words. Newly capable of identifying some of the more basic emotions and of articulating major likes and dislikes, a three-year-old child develops feelings of great intensity and actively seeks to achieve physical and emotional states of preconceived comfort, love, and pleasure.

When your listener reaches the age of three, you can begin to weave more conventional plots, keeping the narrative flow of events simple and direct. "Goldilocks and the Three Bears" is an excellent example of such a story. It reflects a young child's search for "just the right thing" and, in addition, the child's recognition that things come in different sizes, including people. Some of the simpler Bible stories, such as "Noah's Ark" and "David and Goliath" also satisfy this recognition.

Other examples of stories that appeal to the three- to five-year-old age group are formula tales, nonsensical verse stories (like "The House That Jack Built"—a personal favorite—or any of the "Mother Goose" stories), the tales of Beatrix Potter, and stories about holidays, such as tales of Santa Claus, the Easter Bunny, and that expert meteorologist, the groundhog. Stories of this type evenly balance the familiar with the unusual. They present just the right amount of everyday events or phenomena as well as predictable plot progressions blended in with fantastic details and surprising narrative twists to keep children in this developmental stage from becoming either impatient or confused.

Ordinary items that fascinate children of two to five years include holes and puddles, cars, planes and trucks, birds, dogs, cats, and squirrels, rain, snow, thunder and lightning, houses and shops, meals and snacks. Extraordinary items that fascinate two- to five-year-old listeners tend to be variations on the ordinary items: animals that behave like humans, weather that is particulary strong or varied, holes and puddles that are unusually wide or deep, vehicles that are specially equipped to suit a driver's every need, shops and houses that are eccentrically designed and filled with surprising and funny things, meals that mark festive events, and snacks that appeal to different creatures, both human and animal.

Children of two to five years are also fascinated with manipulating their environment. Though they are apt to be unable to appreciate the spectacular nature of magic or transformation that is a principal feature of most folk or fairy tales, they do enjoy stories like "The Three Little Pigs" that explore different ways of approaching the same situation. "The Billy Goats Gruff" is a slightly more complex story about three goats who successively attempt to cross a bridge guarded by a troll that also incorporates a rhythmic and repetitious recasting of circumstances—one that speaks to the heart of the child who is continuously involved in a trial-and-error approach to determining what is the most satisfactory mode of behavior.

The symbolism of "three" is pervasive in stories geared toward this age group for good reason. On the one hand, the child of two to three years is conscious for the first time of past, present, and future. He or she knows there are some points of view that have been outgrown, some that are current, and some that are yet to be attained. On the other hand, the child of two to three years is making his or her first earnest attempts to problem-solve. A story having only two variations on a theme implies an either-or decision-making climate: the implication being that there is one entirely correct way and one entirely incorrect way. Having three variations suggests a more flexible and discriminating arena of choice, one that better represents real-life situations. You could easily go beyond three variations; but three is sufficient, easier to remember, and less inclined to be tedious.

Child psychologist Erik Erikson describes the major developmental issue faced by the two- to five-year-old as coming to terms with the conflict between feeling and doubting one's autonomy. By two and a half years of age, most children have mastered daytime control of their urinary and bowel functions, but they can still feel uncertain about the extent or nature of this mastery for years to come. They are not sure what is theirs, what is not theirs, and what must be shared. Often a child of two or three will refer to himself or herself impersonally as "baby," as in the expression, "Baby want water," or objectively, as in the expression, "Me want water." Children of three to five are fond of creating imaginary playmates— other, complementary, and partially realized selves in whom they can confide and to whom they can exhibit their skills. Listening to a child talk with or about his or her imaginary playmate can give you a number of fruitful story ideas.

It is too early at this point in the child's life to expect him or her to have a strong concept of self-identity: one to which you could appeal in stories that have a hero or heroine who undergoes a change in character, situation, or attitude, like Jack in "Jack and the Beanstalk" or Little Red Riding Hood. In most cases, it is too soon for the child to contemplate the idea of leaving home and having an independent adventure. Storytelling in itself, however, helps children face this conflict between feeling autonomy and doubting it by placing them in a decidedly privileged and self-important role: that of the recipient of special ideas and information, meant just for them, that is unobtainable in any other way.

Good printed sources for special story ideas aimed at a preschool audience include Frederick Richardson's *Great Children's Stories*, Hope Newell's *The Little Old Woman Who Used Her Head and Other Stories*, and Virginia A. Tashjian's *Juba This and Juba That*.

Five to Eight Years Old

When chidren are around four to five years old, they undergo one of the most emotionally demanding and mentally stimulating challenges they will ever know in their lives. Their attention and interest shifts from their digestive areas—the mouth, the bowels, and the bladder—to their genital areas. They feel the first heavy onslaught of their sexuality, and their emerging concept of self-identity becomes inextricably bound with their gender role. They are newly aware of the anatomical differences between boys and girls and men and women, and they begin to envision the opposite sex as "the other." Inevitably this leads to fantasies of a romantic relationship with the parent of the opposite sex.

Sigmund Freud, inspired by two of the most mysterious myths of the ancient Greek storytellers, called this frustrating and guilt-ridden developmental crisis the "Oedipal complex" for males and the "Electra complex" for females. The young son sees his father as a rival for his mother's affections. Subconsciously, he wishes to compete with the father and get him out of the way, just as Oedipus, searching for his true identity, unknowingly fights and kills his father when he reaches a crossroad. The young son also subliminally longs to enjoy the full extent of his mother's womanly love, just as Oedipus, again unknowingly, chooses his own mother as his bride. The young daughter yearns to have her father all to herself. Like Electra, she typically is left alone with her mother while her father goes away; and her sense of a just claim on her father's exclusive attention—as opposed to the unjust claim of the mother, who has already had an extensive life with the father— masks her underlying physical and emotional desire to eliminate her same-sex competition altogether and bind herself forever to the male champion in her life.

Children experience the full range of this dilemma, which is not only a conflict between them and their parent of the same sex but also a conflict within their own minds. They know instinctively that their secret longings are not appropriate to the real world and are not in accord with their already ingrained love and fear of both parents. Eventually they resolve the dilemma to some degree by increasingly identifying with the parent of the same sex and, through this identification, gaining the independence to choose more satisfying outlets for competition and romance. In the meantime, the anxiety-provoking drama continually replays itself within their subconscious minds.

Children around five years old are also just beginning to perceive themselves as functional individuals. This perception is sparked not only by their budding sexuality but by their emerging sociality as well. Accelerated contact with peers, especially as formal schooling begins, helps them form personal aspirations, entertain multiple points of view about the human experience, and wonder and speculate about the possibilities life has to offer. Children at this age start to venture away from the home base and confront new people entirely on their own initiative. Through these adventures and confrontations, they learn to value certain personality characteristics, like friendliness, sensitivity, extroversion, and self-confidence, and to reject others, like selfishness, prejudice, jealousy, insubordination, and tyranny.

As a result of this self-actualizing process, as well as their growing cognizance of such adult-world social problems as overly large families, marital quarrels, divorce, neighborly disputes, troublesome divisions of property, poverty, crime, and violence, children between the ages of five and eight become passionately concerned with the notion of justice. The questions uppermost in their minds are: How can this happen? Is it fair? Will I get what I deserve? Will others get what they deserve? How can things work out for the best?

Children in this developmental stage lack the ability and scope to grapple with these questions rationally for several years to come, just as they cannot yet logically reconcile their psychosexual conflicts with their parents. In the meantime, they are compelled to live a large part of their daily lives in an imaginary world of hope and dread, doubt and conviction, promise and defeat, bliss and terror, change and transcendence. Make-believe stories help them survive while they are in this imaginary world and offer safe passages between that world and the real world.

Thus the years between five and eight are the golden years for storytelling, particularly in regard to fairy tales and folktales, which are singularly effective in symbolically portraying an individual's efforts to overcome life's difficulties. Bruno Bettelheim, in his book *The Uses of Enchantment*, pinpoints this feature of fairy and folktales as a key reason for their popularity with children in this age group:

> The more I tried to understand why these stories are so successful at enriching the inner life of the child, the more I realized that these tales, in a much deeper sense than any other . . . material, start where the child really is in his psychological and emotional being. They speak about his severe inner pressures in a way that the child unconsciously understands, and—without belittling the most serious inner struggles which growing up entails—offer examples of both temporary and permanent solutions to pressing difficulties.

Children from five to eight are busy acquiring specific academic skills. As they are taught how to read and write, they rapidly discover new words that help them express how they feel. For all their progress, however, they also realize how much work is necessary before they can achieve proficiency in using educational tools to cope with their environment. They know it will be several years before they can articulate their most private feelings, and they learn for the first time the intrinsic value of symbols and metaphors to express the inexpressible. The fairy or folktale directly addresses in a nonthreatening manner those complicated and anxiety-provoking aspects of human life that are precisely the ones most likely to remain undiscussed between a parent and a child of this age, for obvious reasons, and yet the ones that most frequently preoccupy that child's unconscious mind.

To the three-year-old, or even the four-year-old, the tale of Hansel and Gretel, for example, may be too disturbing. Children this young may be frightened after hearing the story that their parents will want to get rid of them and put them at the mercy of a fearsome old witch. It is, of course, a "play fright"—no real damage occurs; but it is a reaction that can render the story unenjoyable. To the five-year-old, by contrast, "Hansel and Gretel" can offer immense reassurance. In a sense, he or she has already left home and tasted some of the delights and terrors in the world outside and can identify with almost anyone who does the same. The story helps children of this age believe that if they keep hoping and persevering and cooperating with their allies, they will triumph in the end. It gives them a safe playground in which to experiment with their feelings and to work out conceptual questions of who, what, why, how, when, and where. Children of five to eight appreciate this and often demand stories about frightening monsters, wicked sorcerers, and dark dungeons, as well as stories about beautiful princesses and handsome princes, fabulous treasures, and marvelous inventions.

Apart from any psychological value it may possess, a fairy or folktale is a highly imaginative form of entertainment. In fairy and folktales, we can free ourselves from the limitations of the real world and talk with animals; gain magical control over people, places, and events; experience new customs and rituals; and play with delightful explanations of why things are the way they are.

Children of five to eight are particularly enthusiastic about the entertainment a good fairy tale or a good folktale offers. Through education, they are strengthening their mental powers of visualization and conceptualization; and fairy and folktales are full of images that exercise these powers. They love details that poetically appeal to their inner eye, such as the "fact" that elves wear white when they are sad. They welcome make-believe explanations for why a camel has two humps or what a shooting star means: These explanations temporarily fill potentially paralyzing gaps in their understanding of nature and stimulate their curiosity to learn more about the real answers.

Children in this age group also relish the intricate plot patterns and symbolic rhymes that are characteristic of most fairy tales and folktales, for example, the counterpoint of Rapunzel's long hair and the tall tower in which she is imprisoned. Such details inspire them to seek coordinances and symmetries in the real world, which can otherwise appear chaotic and baffling. Above all, they enjoy heroes with whom they can identify in a very personal manner and who permit them to project their fears and hopes outward, so that they can examine them more objectively.

Andrew Lang has edited a series of books that constitutes perhaps the most widely available and comprehensive collection of fairy and folktales for this age group that we have. The most well-known tales are featured in *The Blue Fairy Book*, but equally interesting and more culturally diverse tales can be found in other "color" books in the series—*The Red, Green, Yellow, Olive, Grey, Lilac, Violet, Rose, Pink, Brown, Crimson, Orange,* and *Rainbow Fairy Books.* The tales amassed by the Brothers Grimm, Charles Perrault, and Joseph Jacobs are also excellent sources for storytelling, as are the less complicated original tales of Hans Christian Andersen and Rudyard Kipling—particularly Kipling's *Just-So Stories.* Seven- to eight-year-olds may appreciate adaptations from the more intricate tales of Hans Christian Andersen, Eleanor Farjeon, Seamus Mac-Manus, Natalie Babbitt, and Diane Wolkstein.

Eight to Twelve Years Old

Children of eight to ten have developed a reasonable amount of confidence in their ability to understand the world around them and to operate successfully within it. Though they may still enjoy fairy tales, they tend to associate the simpler stories with babyness and are ready to listen to more complex adventure stories of romance and intrigue.

Literary fairy tales, like those of Oscar Wilde and Jane Yolen, appeal to anyone from age nine onward and can easily be adapted for storytelling purposes. More sophisticated folktales, particularly ones that illuminate the listener's own cultural background or the cultural background of other ethnic, national, and religious groups are ideal for this age group. Harold Courlander is perhaps the most popular anthologist of this type of folklore, especially in terms of African, Indonesian, native American, and Afro-American tales. Ethel Johnson Phelps' *The Maid of the North* offers a collection of twenty-one traditional tales about nontraditional heroines from a wide variety of cultures. Other works to investigate include those of Richard Chase, Jack Lester, Parker Fillmore, and Peter and Moe Absjornsen. Children of ten to twelve are ready for oral versions of stories by Washington Irving, Edgar Allan Poe, and Isaac Bashevis Singer.

Of Children and Tales

Deeper meaning
Lies in the fairy tales of my
  childhood
Than in the truths that life has
  taught.
—FRIEDRICH SCHILLER

Little Red Riding Hood was my first love. I felt that if I could have married Little Red Riding Hood, I should have known perfect bliss.
—CHARLES DICKENS

My first and last philosophy, that which I believe in with unbroken certainty, I learnt in the nursery. . . . The things I believed most in then, the things I believe most now, are the things called fairy tales.
—G. K. CHESTERTON

We begin by telling children stories which, though not wholly destitute of truth, are in the main fictitious. . . . The beginning is the most important part of any work, especially in the case of a young and tender thing; for that is the time at which the character is being formed and the desired impression is more readily taken.
—PLATO

The wonder is that the characteristic efficacy to touch and inspire deep creative centers dwells in the smallest nursery fairy tale—as the flavor of the ocean is contained in a droplet or the whole mystery of life within the egg of a flea.
—JOSEPH CAMPBELL

Living things, moving things or things that savor of danger and blood, that have a dramatic quality, these are the things natively interesting to children, to the exclusion of almost everything else, and the teacher of young children, until more artificial interests have grown up, will keep in touch with his pupils by constant appeal to such matters as these.
—WILLIAM JAMES

When my cousin and I took our porridge of a morning, we had a device to enliven the course of a meal. He ate his with sugar, and explained it to be a country continually buried under snow. I took mine with milk, and explained it to be a country suffering gradual inundation. . . . But perhaps the most exciting moments I ever had over a meal

were in the case of calf's foot jelly. It was hardly possible not to believe—and you may be quite sure, so far from trying, I did all I could to favor the illusion—that some part of it was hollow, and that sooner or later my spoon would lay open the secret tabernacle of that golden rock. There, might some Red-Beard await his hour; there might one find the treasures of the Forty Thieves.

—ROBERT LOUIS STEVENSON

Storytellers make us remember what mankind would have been like, had not fear and the failing will and the laws of nature tripped up its heels.

—WILLIAM BUTLER YEATS

A good story has the same effect on me that I suppose a good drink of whiskey has on an old toper—it puts new life in me.

—ABRAHAM LINCOLN

Children in this developmental stage are typically fascinated with magic and delight in pondering questions about the limits of possibility: How far can one go with a given amount of resources? How powerful can one conceivably be? How much can exterior forces—like secret languages and rituals—affect people against their will? While children of five to eight seek story heroes with whom they can immediately identify in some way or another, children of eight to ten seek heroes who are greater than they are, embody attributes to which they can aspire, accomplish supernatural tasks, and are capable of serving as symbolic role models in their transition to the adult world. Because of this, myths and legends have a special significance for them. At the ages of eight and nine, children are most likely to enjoy yarns about such legendary figures as Paul Bunyan, Robin Hood, Calamity Jane, and Davy Crockett, and stories featuring the less complicated mythic heroes, like Perseus, Jason, and Theseus in Greek mythology. They are also a prime audience for ghost stories: tales that tease their expectations and confound their senses. From nine to ten, they are ready to hear about the exploits of the gods and near-gods, myths that explain the origin of the earth and the seasons, and stories about more complicated mythic heroes like Odysseus in Greek mythology and Siegfried in Scandinavian mythology. From ten to twelve, they are able to appreciate the narrative and philosophical complexities of such sagas as the Trojan War and King Arthur's Round Table.

Children from eight to twelve are developing their powers of reason and judgment and are typically concerned about the extent of their own competencies. The modern lack of a mythology to which they can refer for symbolic guidance and against which they can imaginatively measure their achievements makes storytelling at this age a crucial developmental need. Most parents today are unable to inspire their children to great deeds by passing along heroic accounts of their ancestors or to offer their children vital links to the natural world around them by reciting popular articles of faith and belief. In many cases, the child has very limited experience with land in its natural state. Even more problematic is the fact that a great number of loving and honorable parents in today's increasingly secular society cannot truthfully or comfortably share personal accounts of spiritual experiences. It is no wonder then that science fiction exercises such a strong hold over children from the ages of eight to twelve, and you may want to explore science fiction tales for storytelling in addition to tales from the mythologies and legends of different cultures. Look for literary accounts of myths and legends rather than encyclopedic accounts when you are searching for good story ideas. Children aged eight to twelve are typically concerned about their own artistic capabilities; and as a result of endlessly sketching cars, spaceships, horses, human profiles, floorplans, or treasure maps, they have a keen eye for detail. They enjoy envisioning what the dragon that guards the sacred tree actually looks like or how a giant could have eyes like millwheels.

Howard Pyle is an outstanding recounter of the legends surrounding King Arthur and Robin Hood, and his works yield many exciting story ideas. Padraic Colum's *The Children's Homer* is a good source of tales from the *Iliad* and the *Odyssey*, and Robert Graves' *Greek Gods and Heroes* offers perhaps the most colorful and comprehensive overview of Greek mythology. For tellable tales from Scandinavian mythology, I refer you to any of the works of Ingri and Edgard d'Aulaire, Margaret Hodges, or Dorothy Hosford. If you wish to investigate science fiction stories, look into the *Star Challenge* or *Doctor Who* series. You can also try borrowing ideas and plots from the following anthologies of adult science fiction magazine stories: *The Best Science Fiction of the Year*, *Nebula Award Stories*, *Science Fiction Review*, *The Best from Galaxy*, *The Hugo Winners*, and *Science Fiction Greats*.

Stories for All Ages

The specific stories or story sources suggested in each section of this chapter represent only a fraction of the material I have found to be effective and that librarians, storytellers, and parents recommend. There are several ways you can easily obtain many more models appropriate to each of the age groups I have discussed.

The first place to check is your local library. By virtue of their education as well as their experience, librarians will be able to help you select stories that have a good chance of appealing to a particular listener based on his or her age group and special interests. They can also assist you in choosing appropriate stories for given groups of people or occasions.

Most libraries have special collections of regional folklore that you can examine as well as storytelling records and tapes and catalogs of children's stories in print. Important anthologies compiled by authorities in the field of children's literature include: *An Anthology of Children's Literature*, edited by Johnson, Sickels, and Sayers; *A Book of Children's Literature*, edited by Hollowell; and *The Arbuthnot Anthology*. If you are interested in finding stories that feature a particular subject you feel your listener may like, such as cats, pirates, snow, or bicycles, try examining the *Subject Guide to Children's Books in Print* for titles.

Some libraries publish recommended story lists, divided according to subject and audience, and conduct storytelling sessions that are open to anyone who wishes to listen. Before dropping into a storytelling session, however, it is wise to let the librarian in charge know in advance and to establish whether the storytelling itself features reading from a book or sharing stories face-to-face.

When checking out books from the library, be sure to include a wide range of types of tales and, if possible, two or three versions of a few of the individual tales. Let your own interests be your guide if you have no other. Although you may be tempted to choose books that have a lot of pictures, remember that your principal need is for the text itself.

Another place to find stories is your local bookstore: the bigger the bookstore, usually, the better. An increasing number of cities have bookstores that specialize in children's literature. Bookstores are wonderful places to get a good general sense of what is currently deemed of interest to children. By browsing through children's nonfiction, science fiction, game, humor, and cartoon books, as well as story books, you can learn a great deal about the popular culture in which school-age children today are growing up. The assortment of storybooks itself will primarily consist of the most recent publications; but a good children's book has a longer life than the average adult book and is usually available for a number of years after its original publication.

Almost every bookstore has a copy of *Books in Print* available to the public; and if you can't find a particular book in stock, you can order it. It is an excellent idea to purchase one or two collections you like. The investment will motivate you to read these books more attentively, and you will always have them around whenever you require them or feel in the mood for exploring. If listeners seem interested in a tale you have told from one of the books, you can share the written version with them and help stimulate their desire to read.

Teachers are experts in choosing appropriate stories for the age group they teach and respond eagerly to outside requests for advice and information. Your listener's teacher is uniquely qualified to suggest subjects, story types, individual stories, and various story-telling approaches your listener will probably enjoy. Any opportunity for a dialogue between a parent and a child is worth pursuing; and by contacting a teacher for story recommendations, you are creating an exchange that will be profitable to all parties involved. Schools, like libraries, often host storytelling events; and the school librarian is liable to be just as helpful to you as the public librarian.

Many cities have folklore societies and museums that offer lists or texts of children's stories. Some societies and museums sponsor storytelling events and lectures about myths, legends, folktales, and fairy tales. Check your phone book or your local chamber of commerce for listings and call or write for informational literature. Also investigate local radio schedules for storytelling programs.

Another option is to write to institutions that promote storytelling and children's literature. Often they can send you lists of tales recommended for different types of listeners, introduce you to national periodicals spotlighting children's stories (such as *The Horn Book Magazine*) and let you know about national and regional storytelling events and organizations, as well as schools that conduct storytelling courses. Among these institutions are the National Association for the Preservation and Perpetuation of Storytelling in Jonesboro, Tennessee 37659; the Office of Children's Services of the New York Public Library at Forty-second Street and Fifth Avenue in New York City 10018; The American Library Association at 50 East Huron Street in Chicago, Illinois 60611; the Children's Department of the Pittsburgh Carnegie Library in Pittsburgh, Pennsylvania 15213; and the Children's Department of the Enoch Pratt Free Library in Baltimore, Maryland 21201.

The final, and potentially most beneficial, recommendation I can make is to ask people (children as well as adults) to tell you their favorite stories: It is not only wise to put yourself in the role of the listener from time to time if you are going to be a teller, but it is also a means of advertising your interest in stories. If you ask one of your potential listeners to tell you a story, you get the best possible evidence of what he or she enjoys.

Pathways To Storytelling

• Keep a daily or weekly journal of what you have observed or thought about a specific child or children in general. If you are a parent, try to reconstruct your child's day, based not only on what you know but on what you imagine. If you don't routinely interact with children, you can build on your memories or on recent incidents that triggered certain insights. You can also try keeping a journal about yourself as if you were communicating with a child. Envision a particular boy or girl as your audience, even if you have no real-life model. Record the day's events in story form. You can do this regularly or occasionally: The important thing is to create a narrative describing events of the day as they happened, without editorial comment. You may find it helpful to write your entry in the present tense, as if you were simultaneously "dreaming" of what happened that day.

• Browse through the childhood portions of biographies and autobiographies. Frequently they contain marvelous anecdotes that reveal much about the point of view of a child. They can also provide you with specific story ideas. I particularly enjoy the recorded childhood memories of people who grew up to become, in some sense, storytellers: Charlie Chaplin, Winston Churchill, Walt Disney, Helen Keller, Agatha Christie, and so on.

• Read books about children: especially ones that will give you a sense of how they think, what occupies their minds, what they like and dislike. I find Penelope Leach's *Birth to Age Five* and Selma Freiberg's *The Magic Years* particularly helpful for understanding younger, less verbal children. It is also fun and informative to read adult fiction that succeeds in communicating the sensibilities of children. Among the most effective works in this genre that I have discovered are Ray Bradbury's *Dandelion Wine*, Steven Millhauser's *Edwin Mullhouse*, Henry James' *What Maisie Knew*, and that wondrous extended fairy tale, James Stephens' *The Crock of Gold*.

CHAPTER FOUR

REMEMBERING AND ADAPTING STORIES

We have all had the experience of wishing we could think of a good joke to pull out at a party or a clever anecdote to share when we are alone with a stranger. Jokes, anecdotes and, yes, children's stories have a unique charm because they take us a step away from the mundane, the predictable, the habitual.

Although becoming a successful jokespinner or raconteur or storyteller is not as complicated as becoming a good actor, it is still entering into a land of make-believe; and we need to know where we are going when we do that. We are no longer in the real world, where we are pushed forward by routines, only half-thinking about what we are doing, or saying, or being. Instead, we are in a world for which we need special preparation—an internalized set of directions and the right equipment for the circumstances we may encounter. The more we prepare ahead of time, the more comfortable we will be in that world.

One major difference between telling a story and telling a joke or an anecdote is that in telling a story you have more material and more devices to help you out. A joke or an anecdote is a tightly condensed exhibition piece compared to a children's story. Every phrase needs to be memorized, and you must slip the whole works quickly and forcefully into a running, real-world conversation that competes with it. The beauty of storytelling is that you have the time, the space, and the climate to relax. You and your listener have already become traveling companions before you even begin to tell your story. You are the conveyer of moods, characters, and events rather than the performer of a script who must assume a role (or a number of roles) and guard against making any false steps.

Learning a story is a matter of being certain you can make your way, given your company, from one landmark to another. And there are several tacks you can take.

The simplest method is to read the complete story several times in a row before you tell it. If it is a story you have made up in advance, write it down, however sketchily, so that you can do this. Some storytellers write (or type) a story even if it already exists in printed form. The activity of personally reproducing the story helps them remember it; and in the process, they can simplify or adapt the original version if it doesn't quite suit their needs or preferences.

I prefer five readings; I love to read and give myself enough time to dwell within the framework of a story for a while. You may want to follow my pattern until you devise one that fits your personal temperament.

Reading for enjoyment

On the first reading, simply concentrate on whether you enjoy the story. You don't have to like every part of the story: Maybe a detail that doesn't particularly move you will stir the imagination or interest of your listener. You can also adapt details later to match your taste or the taste of your listener. What is crucial is that you respond favorably to the story as a whole. Ask yourself whether you like the rhythm of the plot and whether it leaves you with a heightened sense of joy, wonder, compassion, curiosity, or understanding. Try to express to yourself what, in particular, makes the story appealing to you.

Reading for character study

On the second reading, think about the personalities of the characters, as you perceive them. Consider not only what their actual words and behavior say about them but also what images take shape in your mind when you try to imagine what the characters are like.

You may envision one of Cinderella's stepsisters, for example, as a stylishly dressed girl who is immaculately groomed—constantly endeavoring to make the most of a long neck and graceful hands and to downplay a mottled complexion and a low forehead. Maybe she doesn't smile because she has bad teeth, and she never takes a clear look at what is happening because she is nearsighted. She is so busy with herself that she has no time to care about others. You may want to call her "Pristella," a name that connotes prissiness.

Perhaps you see Cinderella's other stepsister as pretty but deliberately mean—suspicious of anyone else whose beauty might compete with hers. She cares much less about clothes and makeup, and much more about rights and power. You may want to call her "Emporia," a name that connotes pompousness.

Maybe you can think of a person you know or a performance you have seen in the movies or on TV that you can mentally associate with a story character. The activity of giving story characters appropriate personalities in your mind will help you remember the story as a whole more easily, give you confidence that you understand the motives of the principal players, and make your ultimate delivery of the story more well rounded.

The purpose of giving yourself a better sense of the characters' personalities is not necessarily so that you can talk more about them. Children are apt to get bored with lengthy descriptions of characters. Instead, the purpose is to make what you do say about the characters more revealing.

For example, knowing what you know about Cinderella's stepsisters, you may want to have Pristella squint at Cinderella whenever she speaks to her; and you won't have to mention the potentially irrelevant fact that she is nearsighted. By contrast, Emporia can open her eyes wide and stare directly at Cinderella, a gesture that is more in keeping with her character: something, again, you don't need to point out. As they leave for the ball, you can have the first stepsister stopping for one last look in the mirror and the second stepsister leaping ahead to get the best seat in the carriage. Your listener will inevitably pick up a consistent difference between the way the two characters operate, which is far better than your summarizing the basic nature of that difference.

Reading for catchwords and transition phrases

Once you have a working sense of the personalities of the characters, read the story a third time and memorize special catchwords and transition phrases: ways of saying things that you do want to preserve, however you adapt the story, and that can function as cues for remembering what comes next. To recapture the story "Jack and the Beanstalk," for example, you may want to memorize an expression of Jack's mother you find especially colorful, such as, "Oh Jack, you troublesome scamp of a son"—an expression you can repeat whenever Jack's mother addresses him. Or you may want to memorize the phrase, "That night as the round, golden moon cast its full light on the magic beanstalk," because it will prompt you to switch to the scene where Jack begins to climb.

The third reading is also an excellent occasion to divide the plot into its component parts. Ask yourself, What are the major events, in order? How does each event begin and end? Where, precisely, are the "break-points?" You may want to create a tag word for each event: a code to enable you to recall the event more easily.

For example, a mental list of the events occurring in the story, "Owl," could read as follows:

1. Owl thinks he's ugly; night meeting with girl; "If the sun had been shining . . ."
2. Evening visits; mother's question; party plans
3. Owl scared; asks Cousin Rooster; "I can't go on . . ."
4. Sun sets; Owl comes; "Haven't you ever seen a hat before?"; Rooster's promise to crow
5. Girl and Owl dance
6. Owl hears crowing too late; mother removes hat; "MY EYES!"; "Wait please, Owl!"; noblest face
7. Owl never returns; girl marries Rooster—when she hears him crow, wonders about Owl

Reduced to personally meaningful tag words, this list might become as abbreviated and easy to recall as the following list:

1. meeting
2. mother
3. Rooster

4. hat
5. dance
6. eyes
7. marriage

You don't need to be as specific or formal in your observations on this third reading as I am being here. You don't have to write anything down. Simply be aware of the plot's structure.

Reading for environment

During the fourth reading, concentrate on the physical setups of the story: the buildings, rooms, and furnishings; the landscapes, waterscapes, and weather; the clothes, tools, and talismans. Ask yourself questions such as, What type of den does Mole inhabit? What would a map of Neverneverland look like? How would Joseph's coat of many colors feel? How would the cry of a banshee sound?

Maybe the hero of the story performs a simple household task that is unfamiliar to you or that your reader may not know. If you want to make a strange custom, object, or belief more distinct, you can alter it into something more common or do some quick research to find out more about it. Sometimes a short, conversational explanation of a little-known fact provides an effective introduction to storytelling.

When I was a summer-camp counselor in southern Ohio, I once decided to tell a native American tale that involved a turtle to an eight-year-old audience fascinated with turtles. I was fairly sure that most of them had not examined turtles very analytically; and I was positive that none of them knew much about the native American lunar calendar. As luck would have it, turtles flourished in our usual storytelling spot by the river. I held one up and pointed out that it had thirteen big squares on the back of its shell—as turtles always do—and that this can be taken to represent the thirteen moons in the year. I also showed them the twenty-eight smaller squares around the larger ones, which can be taken to represent the number of days in the lunar cycle. A smooth transition to the tale itself was easy.

Before you begin the story "The Laziest Lass in Ireland," you may want to talk about how clothes were made in the past, to render the flax, the spinning, and the weaving more vivid to the listener.

An Earth-shattering Memory Technique

Twenty-four hundred years ago a tragic event on the Greek island of Ceos inspired the famous orator Simonides to invent a memory technique that storytellers have used for centuries to remember their tales.

One evening, while Simonides was attending a banquet, a devastating earthquake struck. He survived unharmed, but many of the guests still reclining at the table were crushed to death beneath heavy stones and mutilated beyond recognition. Simonides was the only one who could identify the corpses because he happened to recall which couch each person had been occupying.

The experience was naturally quite upsetting to Simonides; but in true Greek fashion he abstracted a general principle from what had occurred: namely, that memory works by association and that one can create associations to strengthen specific memories.

The first step in Simonides' technique is for a storyteller to envision each of the main chronological events of a story in the form of a separate, concrete visual image. Then the storyteller takes the first image and mentally attaches it to a specific place in a familiar room. Using this as a beginning point, he or she continues around the room, distributing the images in a succession of particularly memorable places. Later, when the storyteller is actually relating the story, he or she can remember its main events in their proper order by taking a mental walk around the room and revisualizing each image in turn.

For example, to remember the main events of the tale, "Raven and the Ball of Daylight," you can create this list of images:

dark world
Chief of Sky's house
spruce needle
baby playing with ball
ball rolling out door

Then you can summon up the image of a familiar room. Suppose it has a clock in one corner. Farther right is a bookcase. Farther right is a chair. Farther right is a table. Farther right is a window.

Given your list of items, you may imagine that the clock has a map of the world, with all the continents in black, superim-

posed on its face. Turning to the bookcase, you may imagine that it rests on a cloud and that the shelves are different stories in a palace. Turning to the chair, you may imagine a slipcover decorated with the image of a spruce needle. Turning to the table, you may imagine a baby playing with a ball underneath it. Turning, finally, to the window, you may imagine that you see a ball rolling out of a door in a building across the street.

After spending several seconds concentrating on each image, you can fix them all, in order, in your conscious memory for an indefinite period of time. You can apply the same technique by imagining key images placed along a familiar route you travel and then visualizing that route from time to time as you are telling the story from which those images are drawn.

When you do this, be brief and be careful not to give any details of the story away. For example, in explaining spinning, you would not want to add, "and sometimes a person's foot would swell from pounding the treadle so much."

Your clear sense of the physical universe through which the characters move will flavor your story, whether or not you consciously apply that sensitivity when you tell the story. You will know where you are going, and that is what is important.

Reading for reassurance

The fifth reading is, for me, the most enjoyable one. I get the same pleasure from it that I get from revisiting, after an extended absence, a strange place I had liked. I have had a chance to think about it—consciously and unconsciously—in a variety of different ways, and now I can approach it more confidently, armed with all I understand about it.

The fifth reading also does the most to guarantee that I remember the story. It sows into the story all I have thought about it in previous readings. It completes a circle. If you don't choose to read a story five times, because you tire of reading or lack the time, read it at least three times: once to know it, once to ponder it, and once to reexperience it, based on your pondering.

Rehearsing the story

After you have finished your last reading of the story, practice telling it aloud, without looking at the text. Imagine you are sharing it with a listener. Do not interrupt yourself or quit or go back. Do not race through it or allow a lot of time between phrases so that you can memorize them as you go along. Your objective is to see if you can re-create the essence of the tale for someone else, not to prove to yourself that you can repeat by heart what you have read and devised. Every time you tell the story it will be different. That is the hallmark and the magic of storytelling.

This auditory approach to remembering a story complements the visual approach of reading and imagining it. It gives you an opportunity to hear the sounds of the words and feel the pace of the narrative line. You will probably discover that when you put the story into spoken words, you automatically come up with fresher, more natural ways of expressing certain things; and you will inevitably train your mind to react correctly to specific rhythmic and aural cues. Telling a story aloud, rather than reading it to yourself, also gives you a much better sense of how long it is.

If you find through rehearsing the story that you have not yet mastered it to your satisfaction, reread the story again and focus on retaining those elements you don't want to forget when you share it with others. Then you can retell the story aloud to assure yourself that you can pass it along in your own language.

Keeping a written record of stories

To supplement your readings of a story, you may want to make brief notes that will help you to recall it at a later date. Keeping a written record of the stories you like is especially wise once you begin accumulating a large repertoire of different types of tales and a wide variety of regular listeners.

For each story you wish to remember, write down the following items in any order, depending on what is most relevant for your needs, as long as you retain the same order for every entry:

Title
Every story needs to have a title for easy recall and reference, including stories you create on your own. It is a good idea to tell your listeners the title of the story you are going to share with them, so that they can remember it more easily too.

Author and/or Source
Many of the best stories for children have no single, recognized author: "Cinderella," "Rumpelstiltskin," and "Sleeping Beauty" are well-known examples. Do not confuse the collector of a tale with the author of that tale. The Brothers Grimm, for instance, did not write a single children's story, although they collected hundreds of them.

The value of identifying the author of a story is that you can look for other stories by the same author—stories that are likely to possess some of the same qualities as the story you discovered and enjoy. Your listener may express interest in a particular tale you have told, which will further motivate you to do this.

The same holds true for identifying the story's source. The source of a story can be any one of a number of items. Maybe it is the book in which you found the story. If that book came from the library, it is a good idea to jot down the call number or classification symbols, so that you can easily retrieve the book if necessary. Maybe you will want to record the name of the person who collected the tale or the name of the storyteller who first told it to you—along with the date of the event. In some cases, it may be appropriate to make notes about the history of the story: the culture from which it came or the circumstances that contributed to its popularity.

Contents

Depending on the story itself, or your individual preference, this entry can include any one or more of the following items: a brief, one-line synopsis of the plot, such as you would find in a newspaper blurb about a television show or movie; the story's main subject; who the characters are; a list of events or tag words, such as I mentioned above; singular phrases, rhymes, or scraps of dialogue you wish to retain; your own shorthand comments about the essence of the story—what you like about it, what its basic mood and key symbols are.

Audience

Write down the type of listener the story may interest—based either on what you have read or heard about the story (often the source of the story will give you clues) or your own gut feeling. You may also want to keep track of your own successive tellings of the story: individuals with whom you have shared it, what the circumstances were, how you think it was received, anything you learned, or tried out, during the telling.

Some people like to keep a file box of stories, with a separate card for each story. Others prefer a loose-leaf notebook. Some people organize their entries alphabetically according to title; others, according to subject matter or type of tale or audience. If you are just beginning to collect stories, it doesn't matter how you keep your records for a while, although it is practical to use a separate card or page for each story. Browsing through your notes to find an individual story may help you to reacquaint yourself with stories you may otherwise forget. Eventually, however, you will want to categorize your entries for more convenient reference. By that time, you will know the way that best fits your situation, and you can simply fill in the top line of each entry to correspond to your chosen system and rearrange your cards or pages to comply.

Adapting stories

Whether you follow a system to remember a story or simply recall a story naturally, you are already adapting that story. It is an experience you have had. And in recounting that experience to yourself or to others, you are the author. You speak in the language you normally use, except, possibly, for certain intriguing words featured in the original story that you may want to repeat; and you describe events as you encountered them. The result is inevitably an adaptation.

Preparing to tell a story is like preparing to ice-skate (It is snowing outside my window as I write this). Before we ice-skate, we watch and we practice. Then, one day, we check the weather and the ice, bundle up accordingly, and strap on our skates. Fortunately, preparing for storytelling comes more easily. Throughout our lives, all of us, even Olympic ice-skaters, have accumulated far more watching and practicing experience relevant to storytelling than we have to ice-skating. Life itself has already put us through basic training in telling stories once we begin to speak: Continued practice is a matter of enhancing skills rather than acquiring them. Actually telling a story is like actually ice-skating. You merely express yourself—you let your talent, your memory, and your vehicle take you along. Each time you tell a story, like each time you skate, it will be unique, whether you intend it to be or not. Children are acutely sensitive to this and often ask to hear the same story again and again, knowing the story will still seem fresh each time it is told.

You may consciously choose to adapt a tale—either in advance or while telling it—so that it will more comfortably fit your own style and understanding, the mood and interests of your listener, and/or the circumstances of the moment. When you do this, you need to respect the essence of the story—what it means to you, what you like about it—and preserve the fundamental elements in the story that give it its special quality: the overall plot, the major characters, and the general environment. When you actually tell the story, you are reliving it and you have the freedom to relive it as you wish. The more thought and care you give to your adaptation, the more you will enjoy displaying it to someone else.

One of the stories I have enjoyed tinkering with the most is "The Star Maiden," a native American tale I heard several years ago on a record made by Anne Pellowski, a storyteller for the New York Public Library. The following summary is drawn from a rough transcript of that recording and does not reflect the full beauty of the original; nor can the fact that I frequently adapt it be attributed to any perceived "faults" in the story. Its very richness invites adaptation.

THE STAR MAIDEN

Once upon a time there lived a young Indian named White Hawk, who was the most skillful hunter of his tribe. One day, while walking across a clearing, he noticed a circle in the grass. It appeared that steps had worn a path in the shape of a ring, yet White Hawk saw no path leading to or from the circle. Certainly this was a magic circle. "If I hide myself and watch," he thought, "maybe I can find out how the ring was made." He lay down in the tall grass and waited.

Soon White Hawk heard distant sounds of sweet music. Looking up, he saw an object descending from the sky. At first it looked like a speck, but it grew larger and larger as it came nearer, and the music became sweeter and sweeter. It was a basket car made of rushes and inside were twelve lovely maidens, the fairest his eyes had ever beheld.

When it landed, the maidens came out and danced round and round it, at each step touching a shiny ball with their feet. The maiden who seemed to be the youngest pleased White Hawk the most. He sprang forward that he might take her hand; but the very moment that he appeared, the twelve sisters took fright and leapt into the basket, which rose in the air until it was out of sight.

White Hawk's heart was sad. "I'll return tomorrow," he said to himself, "and maybe that basket will come back." His eyes fell on a hollow tree trunk nearby. Field mice were scurrying to and from the trunk as if it were their home. "I'll turn myself into a little mouse," he thought. "Such a tiny creature will scarcely be noticed." He moved the trunk as close to the magic ring as he dared. Then he returned to his lodge and waited anxiously for the next day.

As soon as the first rays of the sun appeared, White Hawk ran to the trunk and turned himself into a mouse. Toward evening, he heard music again and saw the basket descending. Again the maidens jumped out. One of them noticed the trunk. "Look," she said, "this trunk was not here yesterday." The others laughed and several struck the stump with their feet. Mice came running out, and the sisters chased them. White Hawk quickly put himself in the path of the youngest maiden and she pursued him far into the woods. She was on the point of striking him with a stick when he changed back into his true shape and caught her in his arms. The others, seeing this, fled back to the basket and rose in the air. The youngest maiden looked longingly after them. White Hawk wiped her tears and told her stories of the wonderful adventures she could have on earth. His heart glowed with joy when she consented to enter his lodge; and from that moment on, she was his bride.

Winter and summer passed and White Hawk's happiness increased when their son was born. But the daughter of the Star Chief, now called Star Maiden, began to yearn again for her home in the sky. She was obliged to hide her feelings, but she remembered the charm which could carry her back. She started making a wicker basket while her husband hunted, hiding it each day near the magic circle. When the basket was finished, she put it into the ring, climbed into it with her baby son, and sang her song. The basket rose up. The wind carried the music to her husband's ears. He knew what it meant and ran to the circle, where he watched the basket until it became a small speck and disappeared.

White Hawk mourned his loss through long winters and long summers. Star Maiden was so happy she almost forgot she had a husband, until her son begged to visit the place where he was born. Star Chief said to them, "Go and ask White Hawk back to live with us. But tell him he must bring a token of every kind of bird and animal which he kills in the hunt." Star Maiden took the boy and descended.

White Hawk heard the music as she came down and hurried to the magic ring. The basket landed, his wife and son jumped out, and he rushed up and embraced them. Star Maiden told him what her father had said, and White Hawk spent whole days as well as whole nights in search of every curious and beautiful animal he hunted. At last he was ready and returned to the sky with Star Maiden and their son.

There was great joy on their arrival. The Star Chief invited all his people to a feast. After they had eaten, he bade each guest choose one item from the pile of items White Hawk had brought. Some chose a foot, some chose a claw, some chose a wing. Immediately, each person was changed into the animal he or she had chosen—and they scattered off in all directions. White Hawk chose the feather of the white hawk, his family emblem. His wife and child did the same. They spread their wings and, with the other birds, descended to earth, where they can be found to this day.

This is the first story I ever told to my niece, Mandy, who is five years old. Since Mandy is very much a little princess herself, I wanted the Star Maiden character to stand out more prominently. After the basket disappeared the first time, I had White Hawk exclaim, "I'll return tomorrow, and maybe I will see the beautiful maiden again." I made her the one who noticed the trunk and who kicked it to send the mice scampering out. I added a detail about all the villagers loving her for her beauty, skill, and kindness and performing a special ceremony to name her "Star Maiden." I gave her a song to sing when she wanted to make the basket move, which was repeated three times in the course of the story (when she returned to the sky with her son, when she brought her son to earth, and when she went back to the sky with her husband and son):

> Rest no more, and bear me yonder,
> With the will of Star Chief, wander;
> Take me safely, ever-tending,
> Where my secret thoughts are bending.

I also let Star Maiden choose the white hawk feather first, to demonstrate more dramatically her love for her earth family.

On other occasions I have made different kinds of adaptations:

- On a Halloween weekend, I changed the basket car into a magic globe resembling a pumpkin, with magic designs carved into the shell. The pumpkin opened into sections so that the maidens could easily step out of it. When Star Maiden wished to return to the sky with her son, she fashioned a huge basket that looked like a pumpkin, with separate sections that could be joined together and magic designs in the weaves. Transit to and from the earth was only possible during the harvest month of October.

- Faced with a particularly intelligent and skeptical eight-year-old, I decided to change White Hawk's strategy for capturing the beautiful maiden into something more rationally ingenious. When White Hawk first saw the sisters, I had him notice that the youngest was the first to jump out of the basket and the last to jump in, and that she looked at the forest about her with curiosity as she danced, unlike the others. After the basket ascended, White Hawk created a special disguise so that if he wore it and stood motionless, he resembled a wondrous tree. On the trunk of the tree, he painted a picture of the beautiful maiden. When the basket landed the next day, the younger sister could not resist stepping outside the circle and wandering toward the tree, which she considered to be equally magic. The other sisters tried to call her back. When she reached the tree, two of its branches—in fact, White Hawk's arms—encircled her.

• Once I was telling the story to the son of parents who I knew were strongly opposed to killing animals. When it came to the Star Chief's message, I had him say, "Bring to me a token of every animal in your forest, but do no harm to any of them." So White Hawk collected the shed skins of snakes, the dropped feathers of birds, paw and hoof prints (which he preserved in clay pots on which he drew the appropriate animal), fish fossils, clumps of fur from branches, spiders' webs, nests, honey, and so on.

• For a storytelling session under an open sky I wanted to emphasize the stars and the hawks. I altered the number of sisters to seven (for the Seven Sisters or Pleiades star cluster in the Taurus constellation); and, when it came to the Star Chief's message, I had him say, "Bring to me a token of the most splendid animal of all animals in your land." White Hawk wandered throughout his land, observing the grace of the deer, the fierce majesty of the bear, the silvery sheen of the trout, the magnificent markings and tail of the fox, the bright colors of the butterfly. Finally, he settled on the white hawk, his family emblem, as the most splendid of all animals. When he presented a white hawk feather to fulfill his bargain, the Sky Chief asked his daughter and grandson if the white hawk is, indeed, the most splendid of all animals. They said yes; and so the Sky Chief waved the feather over White Hawk, Star Maiden, and their son and they were changed into the most splendid white hawks of all.

Through every adaptation of "The Star Maiden," I try to leave the essential structure of the tale intact and to reinvoke the aspects I enjoyed when I first heard it. Among these aspects are the shape-changing, the special powers of Star Maiden—to dance, to weave, to chant—the patience of White Hawk, the mysteriousness of the marriage, the unexpectedness of the ending.

Often my adaptation is partially an effort to make the story mean more to me, personally, by enhancing something I like about it. Sometimes this is a conscious effort; sometimes not. For example, I love the metamorphosis at the end of the story; but, as the story stands, it is only the second metamorphosis. Part of my mind has always wondered why, if White Hawk can change himself into a mouse, he can't change himself into a hawk and follow the basket. Why do the feast guests need to eat the tokens to be capable of doing the sort of thing that White Hawk can do voluntarily? So, depending on my mood, I occasionally sacrifice the clever mouse plan—as I did when I had White Hawk disguise himself as a tree instead—and make Star Chief the only one capable of effecting a real change of bodily form. By doing so, I heighten the significance of that final transformation.

There are several other guidelines besides holding on to what we like about a story that we need to keep in mind when we adapt children's tales:

Stick to the original sequence of major plot elements.

Whether you lengthen a story or shorten it for a particular retelling, follow the same order of key events and revelations that exists in the original version. After all, the original story either evolved or was composed to produce a certain special effect, and that effect can be lost if you haphazardly rearrange things.

For instance, when you tell the story of "Owl," you will want to save any description of how Owl's face really looks until the girl finally sees it the morning after the party, just as it happens in the original tale. Otherwise, you spoil the dramatic surprise of her judgment toward the end of the story that Owl's face is "the noblest face she ever saw."

We have already considered the significance in children's tales of having three trials, instead of just two, before a satisfactory resolution is achieved. It symbolizes a more gradual and varied approach to success. In fact, there is usually a good reason behind the particular number of similar events occurring in a given story, whatever that number may be—a reason we can discover if we examine the story closely enough.

For example, in the tale "Spider and the Box of Stories," Spider is asked to perform four tasks: capturing a python, a leopard, a hornet, and a creature none can see. All are dangerous creatures in very different ways. Each conquest demands a separate kind of trickery and reveals a little more about the way Spider's—and any would-be story-possessor's—mind must work. And, in a tale that has such a strong sense of geography, the location of each capture serves a thematic purpose: one on the ground (the python), one below the ground (the leopard), one above the ground (the hornet), and one on a somewhat fourth-dimensional plane (the creature none can see).

If you detect any such deliberate series of events, be careful about deleting one of the components of that series. You may be inadvertently robbing the story of one of its important points. Whether you make the overall story longer or shorter, try to maintain the same balance of attention to each event that exists in the original, and watch out for adding an event to a series that merely duplicates the nature of an event that is already present.

As long as you follow the order of the major plot elements, which is easier to ensure if you have created tag words to remember them, you can safely cut out any distracting subplots or side elements that may be woven into the original version of the story. Such distractions can be particularly troublesome in myths and realistic adventure stories.

Avoid making the story more difficult to understand.

Do not complicate things by adding explanations, motives, or introspective passages. Let the listener think of these things on his or her own. If you change a plot situation, try to make the revised situation no more complicated than the original one.

In many cases, it may be appropriate to recast details in the story so that they are easier to understand. Strike out passages that are confusing. Use direct verbs. Employ repetitive words, phrases, or rhythms. The most common tendency in adapting a story is to simplify it—to make it fit more comfortably inside our heads. Just remember that if a story makes sense to you, it will most likely make sense to your listener. We don't need to talk down to children when storytelling, but we do need to understand the story ourselves, on our own terms.

Enlarge on action rather than description.

If you wish to make a story longer, add more action—other incidents where a character is doing something, or additional tasks necessary for accomplishing a particular goal. A certain amount of description adds flavor to a story; but when it is overused, description can bring the story momentum to a halt.

It is not necessary, for instance, to draw a full picture of what White Hawk or Star Maiden looks like. It may work against the listener's freedom and desire to create his or her own mental images. You may make a suggestion or two, however, especially if it ties in with the story itself. For instance, you may want to add that Star Maiden has hair that is as black as the night sky. A better idea is to have Star Maiden and Star Hawk reveal what they are like by giving them some special gesture or involving them in some suitable activity.

If you want to say something about a character, an event, or a physical detail in the tale, try letting a character say it or at least think out loud about it. It is rather passive, for example, to state that the gremlin wants George for his supper. It is much more active to have the gremlin confront George and roar, "I shall eat you for my supper tonight!"

In whatever fashion you choose to lengthen a story, keep in mind its basic elements, such as the number of principal characters and major events. You can quickly throw a story out of proportion by increasing either number.

A major event can often be modified into an event with a larger number of individual activities. Take, for example, the strategy of White Hawk to capture Star Maiden. When I changed it to a matter of creating a tree disguise, I increased the number of action steps involved for White Hawk without rendering the event itself any more complex. I often expand White Hawk's hunt for animals to include specific things he actually does during the hunt.

Just as a single event in a story can be remodeled into something involving more activity, a principal character in a story can become more multifaceted in adaptations, thus eliminating the need for "new" characters. For example, when adapting "The Star Maiden," it is clearer and more faithful to the story to have Star Maiden assume a larger role among the twelve sisters than to detract from her importance by giving one or more of the other sisters a speaking role or a specific identity.

The more you get to know a story, the more you will take care of it—consciously or unconsciously—in future retellings. And the more you live with a story, the more possibilities you will generate—consciously or unconsciously—for adapting it. Storytelling is, more than anything else, a form of recreation. To share a story with a listener is to re-create it; and any endeavor that offers us a chance to be creative offers us the most joyful responsibility of all.

Pathways To Storytelling

• Jot down a story you have known for a long time. Perhaps it is a widely familiar one like "The Princess and the Pea" or maybe it is an obscure legend you once heard from a friend. Think about the story for a day or two and practice adapting it in various ways so that eventually you have at least two complete versions you like. If it is a commonly known tale, look up different printed versions in the library and jot down details that catch your attention.

• One day in 1980, on the Malta location of the Robert Altman movie *Popeye*, Shelley Duvall (Olive Oyl) was fondly recalling television's *Shirley Temple's Storybook* and the "Fractured Fairy Tales" segment of *Rocky and His Friends* to her co-star Robin Williams (Popeye). "Why isn't anyone making fairy tales on TV anymore?" she asked. "Why don't you do it?" Williams countered. The result was *Faerie Tale Theatre*, a regular program on the Showtime cable network produced by Duvall and featuring such players as Mick Jagger, the Mandarin emperor in Hans Christian Andersen's "The Nightingale"; Joan Collins, the witch in "Hansel and Gretel"; and Christopher Reeve, the prince in "Sleeping Beauty." Pick any children's tale and imagine that you are turning it into a movie or television show. Whom would you cast? How would you map out the major scenes? What would the sets look like? What props would you use? This kind of activity can help you visualize a story and, therefore, remember it better and re-create it more excitingly.

• Maintain an informal journal of the stories you run across—either reading, listening to storytellers live or recorded, conversing with others, eavesdropping, or watching movies or television shows. Simply write down what you like about the story and what you think the main theme of the story was intended to be. Muse about the story. What were the key events? How would you reorganize it for a child listener? What children's tales does the story recall? What do you imagine occurring in the time before and after the story?

• As a mental exercise before telling a story, try to imagine how the story would appear from the point of view of different characters in the story. How would the prince or the stepmother queen relate events in the story entitled "Snow White?" How would the Star Maiden recount the story that is named for her but is told basically from the perspective of White Hawk? Maybe you will stumble on an altogether new tale. Whatever the case, you will gain more knowledge and experience of the primary tale itself.

CHAPTER FIVE

CREATING YOUR OWN STORIES

reative Storytelling is dedicated to my parents. Each one passed along to me a mighty share of stories: stories they had heard, their personal adaptations of stories, and, the most special stories of all, the ones they made up themselves. Their creativity gave life to my own. No better argument exists for the positive power of sharing original stories with a child.

There is no set of general guidelines for creating a story, as there is for selecting, adapting, or delivering a story. Creative ideas grow mysteriously, automatically, and continuously within the human mind, engendered by all that we see, hear, smell, taste, and touch. All we need to do to take advantage of our creative potential is to pay closer attention to those ideas and to translate them into whatever terms we feel will mean something to others.

Kathryn Morton, a writer and a regular critic for the *New York Times Book Review*, says: "Human supremacy may be the result of technology, but technology is, in turn, the product of man's fancy, for the story of mankind is the story of Story itself. . . . What got people out of the trees was something besides thumbs and gadgets. What did it, I am convinced, was a warp in the simian brain that made us insatiable for patterns—patterns of sequence, of behavior, of feeling—connections, reasons, causes: stories. . . . The first sign that a baby is going to be a human being comes when he begins naming the world, demanding the stories that connect its parts."

Eudora Welty, in her book *One Writer's Beginnings*, also describes storytelling as a natural extension of human consciousness: "Children . . . use all their senses to discover the world," she writes. "Then artists come along and discover it the same way, all over again. . . . Writing a story is one way of discovering sequence in human experience. . . . Connections slowly emerge. Like distant landmarks you are approaching, cause and effect begin to align themselves, draw closer together. Experiences too indefinite of outline in themselves to be recognized for themselves connect and are identified as a larger shape. And suddenly a light is thrown back, as when your train makes a curve, showing that there has been a mountain of meaning rising behind you on the way you've come, is rising there still, proven now through retrospect."

What Kathryn Morton and Eudora Welty are both saying is that stories develop inevitably from our perceptions. The only thing that distinguishes a person who actually produces stories from one who does not is that the former has looked into his or her mind and discovered the stories that are there and has made the decision to communicate those stories to others.

Maybe the primary mode in which you are inclined to be creative is not a verbal one. Maybe, instead, you express your creativity in the form of managing your job, or fishing, or playing football, or cooking, or decorating, or gardening, or making love. Whatever your main creative medium may be, it is bound to help you become a creative storyteller. Personal creativity of any kind begins with the type of mental images discussed in the introduction to this book—pictures that form spontaneously in the imagination, triggered by our senses and our memories. These pictures constitute the very essence of stories, no matter how (or if) we ultimately choose to convey them in our day-to-day lives.

My mother's principal creative outlet is visual arts and crafts. When I was a child, she painted murals on the walls of a breezeway that lay between our house and our garage. I spun many stories for myself to explain the images that appeared in those murals. The jungle man lying under a palm tree was transformed repeatedly into a hero taking his rest after accomplishing feats of daring. The jungle woman across from him, whom I associated with the then-popular television character Sheena, Queen of the Jungle, became a wondrously gifted friend of animals and nature. The baseball player astride his flying bat—designed by my mother to symbolize the name change of our local team from the Columbus Bluebirds to the Columbus Jets—was a wily adventurer who made secret scouting trips to Toronto and Havana, cities our team played within the International League. The same imagination that created these murals also created similarly vivid and dynamic tales interpreting such mythic figures as angels and devils, Santa Claus and Peter Cottontail, the tooth fairy and Jack Frost.

My father, by contrast, has always used storytelling as his chief means of creative expression. He provided me with a playfully illuminating counterhistory populated by such relatives as Christopher Columbus Maguire and Michael O'Angelo and was a source of instant story resolutions for any question that teased my child's brain: Why is the grass green? What will happen to me if I do not hold still while my hair is being cut? Why does a song spend three months climbing up the charts to number one and then disappear altogether after a couple of weeks? Why rinse away toothpaste if it is good for your teeth?

Both of them taught me that creativity is sparked by questions. On the most superficial level, these questions are the ones directly or indirectly addressed to us by others or the ones posed by the culture in which we live: for example, the questions I asked my father about things I did not understand, or the questions implicit in the traditions surrounding Christmas and Easter that informed my mother's stories. On a deeper, more productive level, these questions are the ones we ask ourselves. In my mother's case, with the murals, such a question may have been, How do I wish to represent a man and a woman in this particular recreational environment? In my father's case, with the make-believe ancestors, such a question may have been, How can I identify with these famous people? The questioning mind is a mind that is alert to everything it perceives. Our moment-to-moment observations may seem to be random, but they would not have been made if they had not been relevant to other things going on inside our heads. The questioning mind seeks to invest every observation with some degree of symbolic significance—to trace connections, to weave patterns, to create stories.

Coming Up with a Story Idea

Earlier in this book, I stated several questions we need to ask ourselves after we have read or heard a children's tale. The first and most important one is, What do I enjoy about the story? Once we answer that question, we can identify what we feel is the essence of the story—a crucial aspect of the story that we want to get across whenever we tell it to someone else. This "essence" is identical in nature to what I call a "story idea"—the element around which a story originally takes shape. Other people call it the "inspiration," "core," or "controlling image" of a story. In terms of your own potential children's tales, it is something you have sensed and thought about, consciously or not, which quickly translates into story form once you put your mind to it. A story idea may take one word, or a sentence, or a paragraph to express; and it, too, is the answer to a question you ask yourself—about anything you wish.

Most stories stem from thinking about real-life things that are curiosities in themselves—odd news items, strange sights in the street, unusual happenings, uncommon hobbies, eccentric behavior, exotic locales. But even the most apparently ordinary subject can yield a story idea if it is approached in a fresh manner. You don't even need a real-life subject—you can think one up! When you approach a subject, ask yourself the following questions in order to generate story ideas:

What is it like?

A four-year-old boy rushes through your front door and breathlessly announces, "I saw a dragon! I saw a dragon! It was huge and smoke came out of its mouth and it was coming right at me!" You know he did not see a dragon. But *he* knows he did. Had you seen what he saw, you would have called it a horse. But the word "horse" simply does not fit his dramatic sense of how that creature appeared to him at the time he saw it.

Metaphors, creative comparisons between two different things that share common properties, represent imaginative truths and, therefore, are excellent story catalysts. How would you describe your household—as a zoo, a battle zone, an oasis in a desert? When you form such associations, you are communicating the special nature of your household that a factual definition could not begin to capture. And you are on the brink of creating a story.

Several months ago I was undergoing regular acupuncture treatments for sinus pain. During that period I found myself having to explain the basic principles of acupuncture several times to different people. While I was still involved in the treatments, I volunteered to tell stories at a local library to a group of second-graders. Trying to come up with a story idea, I asked myself, What is acupuncture like? It occurred to me that the feeling I had during treatment was one of floating and that the sensation of a needle was like the peck of a bird. When I met with the second-graders, I told them a story about a young man who had aches and pains and wandered from person to person trying to get rid of them. At last he wound up in China, where he met a beautiful young woman who had marvelous medicine birds. She unrolled a large silk carpet and told him to lie down on it, and then she gave a special command to her birds. At once the birds grabbed the ends of the carpet and carried him gently up into the air. They rested him on a cloud and then hovered over his body for several minutes, eyeing it closely. When they magically detected trouble spots on his body, they lowered their beaks and pressed them gently against these spots until all his pain was gone.

They enjoyed the story. I did not have to say a word about acupuncture, which pleased me; it was merely a subject on my mind at the time I was thinking about creating a story. I might have asked myself instead, What is a library like? or What is my nose like? or What is Chinatown like? Any one of these questions would have started me on the way to weaving a story.

What if . . . ?

The minds of children, far more than the minds of adults, are dominated by wishes, hopes, and fears. Anything seems possible, given the extent of what is yet unknown to them. To regain a childlike point of view is to suspend all our adult-world "proofs" and "disproofs" and to live again in a universe where our imaginations are free to wander and where gamelike speculation is serious business.

Some of the most well known works for children are based on the question, "What if . . . ?" J. M. Barrie's play *Peter Pan* explores what would happen if one could choose never to grow up. C. S. Lewis' novel *The Lion, the Witch and the Wardrobe* evolves from the premise, "What if a closet were so deep it never ended but turned into another world altogether?" Steven Spielberg's movie *E.T.* bids all children to consider what they would do if a visitor from outer space suddenly fell into their care. Among the types of tales we have been reviewing in this book, the what-if proposition is perhaps the most pervasive story idea of all: What if animals could talk (as in "Owl")? What if one were to be granted anything one asked (as in "Aladdin and His Magic Lamp")? What if one had to leave home (as in "Hansel and Gretel")? What if there were no sun (as in "Raven and the Ball of Daylight")? What if one does not keep a promise (as in "The Pied Piper of Hamelin")?

Many intriguing what-if story ideas can be derived from what are affectionately known as "old wives' tales." What if some of the superstitions, homespun beliefs, and enchantments that people have fashioned throughout human history really are true? What if eagle tears cure blindness, as the Navajos believe? What happens if a bride-to-be forgets to chant her lover's name backwards when she catches sight of a full moon over her right shoulder? What if a carpenter wants to make sure that his newly built house is free from evil influences? To stir up a story idea, you can browse through collections of old wives' tales, in *The Annotated Mother Goose*, for example, or in Duncan Emrich's *The Hodgepodge Book* and *The Whim-Wham Book*, or you can invent your own.

Old wives' tales pick up where rationality leaves off. They affirm feelings and intentions and renew faith and commitment. But best of all, they inspire innovation. They are to the imagination what hypotheses are to science. It is no wonder they are dear to children and have been preserved by adults through countless generations of storytelling.

How did it come to be?

Myths, legends, and folktales abound with fanciful explanations for why things are the way they are—how the earth, the seas, and the heavens were formed; how animals acquired their distinctive characteristics; how certain social customs arose. Like old wives' tales, these stories provide necessary poetic alternatives to the explanations of logic.

Make up a supernatural reason for why anything is the way it is and you are far along on your way to a finished tale. It is one of the quickest and easiest ways to create a story because it is such an instinctive activity for the human mind to perform.

Dora E. Elam, a third-grade teacher in Boulder, Colorado, once asked her students for their explanations of what causes thunder. Among the ready responses were these:

> Thunder is a cartwheel with a lot of sticks in it falling out.
>
> I think it's a potato bag with potatoes dropping out.
>
> Some people say that thunder is God washing his clothes.
>
> Daddy says it's old man Joe moving his furniture.
>
> Thunder is a volcano in the sky erupting. Or it might be a giant walking across the Milky Way.
>
> It's dogs mumbling to themselves.

The "how did it come to be" story idea does not have to be a wild and woolly one. You can offer a factual explanation in the context of a story that is, in itself, basically fictitious. You can also provide a very low-key, gentle explanation that is not verifiable but is in perfect keeping with the logic of the story as well as with any more accurate explanation. For example, several versions of "The Pied Piper of Hamelin" conclude by saying that the repentant citizens, bereft of their children, set aside land within their town and reserved it for play; and so the park came to be.

What is the situation here?

In the introduction to this book, I spoke about a creative writing experiment involving randomly selected characters, activities, and settings. The experiment was originally designed to stimulate story ideas by inviting the mind to respond to each new combination with the question, What is the situation here?

To perform this experiment on your own, make three different groups of index cards or scraps of paper: one naming a character on each card or scrap (such as a nun, a redhead, a fool, a king, a plumber, an orphan, and so on); one listing an activity (such as gambling, dancing, plotting, drawing, crying, and so on); and one describing a setting—which can be either a time or a place (such as in a forest, on Valentine's Day, on an airplane, in a circus, at midnight, and so on). Then draw a card or scrap from each group. This will give you a basic story setup. You have only to ask yourself, What is the situation here? and you have progressed to a working story idea.

For example, suppose you select "a king," "plotting," "in a circus." You may decide that the king has lost his kingdom to an evil man while he was away and now he has disguised himself as a clown and is planning an act that will expose the evil man when he comes to see the circus. Or you may imagine that the king is sitting in a circus audience watching a beautiful, elusive, and independent aerialist and planning ways to convince her to become his queen.

Another way to stir up story ideas by asking yourself, What is happening here?, is to look at books or magazines with lots of pictures or at albums with old photographs (preferably featuring people you don't actually know). Try to imagine that each picture or photograph is illustrating a story, and then supply that story with your imagination.

You may want to investigate wordless picture books, available in the children's sections of libraries and bookstores. Although these books control your story line to some degree by providing you with a specific chain of images, you can use them to practice varying your point of view or vocabulary. You can also create your own story-telling scrapbook with postcards, magazine cutouts, and drawings. Simply paste into the scrapbook any item that interests you and browse through the scrapbook whenever you want to develop a story idea. You can spin a story either from a single picture or from a random selection of two or three pictures, basing your story events on your choices.

The beauty of the what-is-the-situation-here? idea-prompting question is that you can apply it anywhere, anytime. Simply look out a window, or pause to take in a particular sight while you are walking down the street, or observe others from a distance while you are attending an event. Resist the temptation to arrive at a fast, logical conclusion about what you see, and dwell for a moment on all the possibilities the scene suggests. If, for example, you are gazing into a shop window and you see a reflection of an elephant on the glass, do not dismiss it by saying, "It's painted on the building across the street." Think of it as an elephant inside the window, where, in fact, you see it. If the reflection appears just above a table, contemplate the idea of an elephant on a table.

What shall I title it?

It may seem premature to come up with a title before coming up with a story, but our minds tend to work this way. Our impressions of a person are liable to remain vague until we have a name around which to crystallize them. Random pieces of information only fit together when we create categories by which to arrange them. And it is difficult to sustain thoughts about something over a period of time unless we develop a word or a phrase that sticks in our memory and can conveniently summon up those thoughts.

As a means of provoking story ideas, try applying the question What shall I title it? to major events in your life. Ask yourself, What title would I give to this day? How would I title a description of my childhood? My last vacation? My relationship with a friend? My working life? Once you have a title, you can go on to create any character/plot/environment combination you wish that suits the title. In addition to working with major events in your life, try giving titles to specific incidents you observe, or to daydreams you spin, or to people and places that interest you.

Many good titles for children's stories include one of Kipling's "six honest serving men": What, Why, When, How, Where and Who—"Where the Wild Things Are," "Where the Sidewalk Ends," "The Girl Who Could Not Cry," "When the Wizard Came to Oakville," "How Granny Evers Won Her Medal," "Why the Storks Came to Haarlem." Think of the questions that preoccupy your own mind, such as How can I find peace, excitement, love? Where do mosquitoes go during the winter? What is inside the building around the corner? Think of questions that could preoccupy the minds of children, such as When will I be grown up? Who is the strongest person in the world? Why do men wear ties? Think of questions that animals might wonder about, such as Where does my master go when he leaves the house? How do I know if a creature is a friend or an enemy? Any of these questions can be restated as a title.

Beginnings . . .

In olden times when wishing still helped, there lived a king whose daughters were all beautiful, but the youngest was so beautiful that the sun itself, which has seen so much, was astonished whenever it shone in her face.
—"The Frog Prince," collected by the Brothers Grimm

There was once a merchant who was so rich that he could have paved the whole street with gold, and even then he would have had enough for a small alley.
—"The Flying Trunk,"
HANS CHRISTIAN ANDERSEN

There was once a poor little donkey on wheels. It had never wagged its tail, or tossed its head, or said, "Hee-haw," or tasted a tender thistle.
—"Donkey on Wheels,"
MRS. W. K. CLIFORD

In the High and Far-Off Times the Elephant, O Best Beloved, had no trunk.
—"The Elephant's Child,"
RUDYARD KIPLING

In a certain kingdom, in a certain land, in a little village, there lived . . .
—"Russian Fairy Tales,"
AFANAS'EV

At the time when men and animals were all the same and spoke the same language . . .
—traditional Navajo beginning

Once upon a time—and a very good time it was—when pigs were swine and dogs ate lime and monkeys chewed tobacco, when houses were thatched with pancakes, streets paved with plum puddings, and roasted pigs ran up and down the streets with knives and forks in their backs, crying "Come and eat me!" . . .
—"Jack the Giant-killer," collected by Katharine M. Briggs

. . . Endings

Then he goes out to the Wet Wild Woods, or up the Wet Wild Trees, or on the Wet Wild Roofs, waving his wild tail and walking by his wild lone.
—"The Cat That Walked By Himself," RUDYARD KIPLING

The marriage feast lasted nine days and nine nights. There were nine hundred fiddlers, nine hundred fluters, nine hundred pipers, and the last day and

night of the wedding were better than the rest.
—"Donegal Fairy Story,"
SEUMAS MACMANUS

They lived in peace, they died in peace, and they were buried in a pot of candle grease.
—traditional Bahamanian ending

And Blanchette, the Little Golden-Hood, kept her word. And in fine weather she may still be seen in the fields with her pretty little hood, the color of the sun. But to see her you must rise early.
—"The True History of Little Golden-Hood,"
CHARLES MARELLES

. . . and they all lived happily ever after—even to Frisk, who enjoyed the greatest luxury, and never had anything worse than the wing of a partridge for dinner all the rest of his life.
—"Princess Rosette,"
MADAME D'AULNOY

Perhaps the most efficient way to gain story ideas from titles is to review lists of already existing titles—not only for children's stories but also for books, movies, and television programs aimed at the general public. You can always borrow an interesting title and make up your own story to fit it. Newspaper entertainment sections and movie and television magazines frequently provide story blurbs that can further inspire story ideas.

Shaping Plots

Once you have a story idea, you are ready to cast it into a plot. It could be that your story idea is already developed enough to constitute a plot motif. The word *motif* is directly related to the word *motive* and denotes a situation or idea that is so charged with meaning—either because it is often used or it contains readily apparent dramatic elements—that it immediately suggests a series of interrelated plot scenes. Ever-popular motifs in the plots of children's stories include:

- a sympathetic character in a bad situation
- a warning from an unusual source
- a magic factor that causes a personality change
- a death-bed promise
- a child searching for a lost parent
- a would-be champion seeking to correct a horrible piece of injustice
- an evil character seeking revenge
- the revelation of the identity of a person in disguise
- the redemption of an unpleasant character
- a mysterious power that can cause either fortune or misfortune
- the intervention of magic to resolve a problem
- the reconciliation of enemies
- the effects of a certain lifestyle on a character's body
- the consequences of intractable behavior
- the loss and recovery of a valuable object
- the restitution of a character's, or a place's, deserved state of being
- a quest to discover identity, fame, fortune, or love

Many storytellers have attempted to describe what they feel is the essential plot breakdown of a good children's tale. In fact, each tale winds up having its own unique plot, proceeding logically and imaginatively from the story idea; and it can be intimidating to think that we have to follow a particular preset pattern to produce an effective plot for the stories we create. Nevertheless, it is worth examining what some of these storytellers have said, if only to give ourselves a sharper sense of what goes into fashioning a plot structure.

A. A. Milne, creator of Winnie-the-Pooh, claimed that most stories for children can be reduced to the following sequence of events: "A character resolves to do something, an obstacle arises, and the character attempts to overcome the obstacle. At first, he meets with failure; but ultimately, he is successful."

Joe Heany, an Irish seanachai, asserts, "Good plots for children are about what dangers travelers go through, whom they meet, and how they help to solve their own and other people's problems along the way."

Mala Powers, who operated the "Dial-A-Children's Story" program for New York Telephone in 1980, describes an ideal plot as one that "helps children identify with a positive way of thinking. That is the whole slant—to stress what one individual can do and the work ethic that is involved in accomplishment."

Maurice Sendak, the author and illustrator of many bestselling books for children, catalogs the basic ingredients of a children's story as "a warning to behave, a punishment for failure to do so, and a resolution showing that everything comes out all right in the end."

Richard Abrahamson, a professor of psychology at the University of Houston, says, "Children like episodic plots involving repeated confrontations with a problem by characters who have opposing points of view."

Matthew Tolley, a professional storyteller who performs throughout the United States and Canada, schematizes a typical children's story plot this way: "A is unkind to B; B successfully undergoes some kind of trial, quest, or ordeal and is rewarded; A, jealous, insists on having a go at the same trial, quest, or ordeal; A fails miserably and is punished."

One thing we can definitely learn from these remarks is that a condensed plot outline helps to stimulate our creative thinking. Sketch out the series of events that you feel will best convey your story idea before you begin filling in details of particular scenes or characters. Tinker with the outline to generate alternative plot directions. You may even find you have several potential stories.

Here are some suggestions that will assist you in developing coherent and entertaining plots:

- *Begin quickly and forcefully.* Briefly introduce the main character. Then set up a scene that plunges that character into action and arouses anticipation about what will happen next. Some of the most compelling children's stories accomplish all this in the opening sentence. The writer Joan Aiken's favorite story beginning is an appropriate illustration: "The most memorable day of my life was the one when my father hit me with a haddock."

- *Have your story unfold according to events, not explanations, descriptions, or summations.* Avoid flashbacks or subplots. Think of your story line as consisting of one action episode leading to another action episode. Chance happenings or coincidences are less dramatically engaging than situations that are linked together in a direct line of cause and effect. Suppose, for example, you made up the following story situation: "Omar secretly longed for a magic ship that would take him away to mysterious places. One day a genie appeared to him and offered to grant him whatever he wished." It is much more dramatic to say: "Omar secretly longed for a magic ship that would take him away to mysterious places. One day, he was pretending he was searching for buried treasure in the trash heap in back of his house when he ran across an old lantern. He rubbed it until it reflected the sun in his eyes and made him blink. When he opened his eyes, he saw a genie, who said, 'You have restored the beauty of my lamp and so I will grant you whatever you wish.'" Although you may find it necessary to incorporate some "bridge passages" in your story (for example, in "Sleeping Beauty" one needs to touch lightly on the one hundred years that pass between the time when Sleeping Beauty falls asleep and the prince arrives to awaken her), try to restrict these passages to a minimum and keep the action as continuous as possible.

- *Organize individual scenes around separate confrontations or conflicts.* Every good children's story features some sort of conflict—between one character and another, or between a character and his or her situation or environment, or between two parts of the same character's personality. A good plot arranges matters so that this conflict manifests itself in several different stages or ways, or at several different times. At each manifestation of this conflict, a confrontation is involved. Most often, it is a confrontation involving the main character and one or more other characters, since the meeting of two or more characters possesses a high human-interest value. But the confrontation can also be limited to that between a character and a task. Construct your original story outline so that each item revolves around some sort of conflict or confrontation.

- *Remember that the story itself is the important thing, not any message that can be derived from the story.* Avoid sermonizing in stories, or I-told-you-so's, or pronouncements of what is right and what is wrong. Let events speak for themselves. Do not allow a character's explicit realization of a general truth to be the turning point distinguishing one event from another. The character's behavior change from one scene to another can reflect this more potently than any words or thoughts the character may entertain at a given moment. Consider the prodigal son's transformation and how it is communicated, or the transformation of Ebenezer Scrooge in Charles Dickens' "A Christmas Carol."

- *Keep plot details simple and easy to remember.* If magic rituals, for example, are included in your story, make sure the rules and procedures are clear and consistent. You don't need to go into why a certain type of magic works; you only need to state what is required to make it work. The magic of television provides a useful analogy. You don't have to know why it works to enjoy it; you simply have to plug it in, turn the knob on, and select a channel. However much fun you, as an adult, may have in devising a clever and intricate plot detail, a child is much more interested in being carried smoothly from one story point to another. My desk drawers are full of sheets of paper containing beautifully elaborate plot elements I forced myself to excise from certain stories precisely because they were too obviously show-stoppers.

- *Consider using rhymes, repetitions, and symbol patterns to make your plot more enjoyable.* We have already observed how a symbol pattern of threes can lend a story both variety and a pleasing overall symmetry. In "The Laziest Lass in Ireland," for instance, the expectation that a second and then a third fairy creature may appear can stimulate the listener to pay closer attention to the plot and to look forward more eagerly to how things will eventually turn out. Another type of symbol pattern that can serve a similar function is the recurrence of a specific color at appropriate points in a story: the goldenness of a lover's hair echoed in the goldenness of metal coins and the goldenness of sunshine. Any consistent appeal to the senses of smell, taste, or touch can function as a symbol pattern. Repeating a phrase every now and then—a typical expression of one of the characters or a phrase that reinvokes the particular nature of a task, a place, or an object—creates a rhythm within the story that is comforting and makes the story easier to follow (as well as to tell!). The same goes for rhymes, whether they are contained within a special saying or song a character uses or within the names or descriptions of individual characters, places, or objects.

- *Try to fashion an ending for your story that releases tension and satisfies the listener's sense of justice.* Some people believe that all children's stories should have happy endings. Too often, however, an altogether happy ending is inappropriate for a given story that is nevertheless entertaining to a child and full of valuable material to ponder. Think of most of Hans Christian Andersen's stories, for example; or the vast majority of ghost stories; or folktales such as "Owl" or "The Pied Piper of Hamelin"; or myths such as the one about Prometheus. Children know that life is not full of happy endings; and they can be enormously comforted by hearing a tale that acknowledges this and yet leaves them feeling hopeful and better equipped to face disappointment, fear, and misfortune. Fashion your ending so that all is at peace and each character has undergone a fate that seems appropriate. Children are insistent on seeing that justice is done, in their own lives and within the life of a story. Owl, in the folktale "Owl," undergoes the logical consequence of his actions, and so the tale is satisfying even though it is sad. Many times when I recount "Cinderella," it has not been enough merely to allow Cinderella to be the victor; I am also pressured to deal out loathsome fates to the evil stepmother and stepsisters.

Bringing Characters to Life

Often a story idea is based on a particular kind of character: a vain boy who refuses to wear glasses, one of the three wise men, a girl who can wriggle her ears and make anything she wants appear before her, a monster who longs to be accepted as a human being. But if your original story idea does not contain any specific characters, there are several experiments you can perform to come up with a suitable cast for your tale.

The most vivid characters are those who represent one dominant quality in several different ways, such as the way they live, the way they think and speak, the way they dress, the way they perform tasks, and the way they react to outside events. Decide on the particular qualities involved in your story—qualities that can be expressed through the characters in the story. If your story is a "quest" story, you may want a character who is basically curious pitted against one who is set in his or her ways. You can give the former a long nose, which is always poking into things, and wide eyes, a house full of strange objects that he or she is forever investigating, and dialogue that is full of questions and wonderings. By contrast, you can give the latter a tiny nose and beady eyes, a plain, unadorned house with no windows, and dialogue that is very brief, emphatic, and dry.

The trick is to organize your entire depiction of a particular character around a single, pervasive attribute and yet make the character believable and not flat. You don't have to stress that attribute every time you mention the character. A few simple touches to convey that attribute are enough. The danger lies in giving a character so many attributes that he or she becomes overly complex. A child will have a difficult time relating to such a character, and the characterization may overshadow the action in the story. For the same reasons, it is important not to give a character attributes that contradict each other (unless the story idea itself calls for a character torn between two modes of behavior, in which case you really have two characters, like Jekyll and Hyde).

In special cases, you may want to state a character's attribute directly—either by giving the character a symbolic name or by portraying the character as one who consciously seeks to acquire a certain quality. Take, for example, Andersen's steadfast tin soldier. In several editions of the tale, the title is simply "The Tin Soldier"; but I have always preferred to connect him directly with the quality of "steadfastness." It is a quaint term that only came to mean something to me in the context of the tale itself. I enjoyed repeating the word as a child and associating it with my uncle, who was overseas participating in the Korean War at the time. Frank L. Baum's cowardly lion seeking courage represents a highly successful allegorical application of the virtue of courage in the context of a children's story. Be careful, however, not to state attributes so directly unless it clearly serves the main theme of your story.

Snow White's name implies all about her character that we need to know—she is virginal and she is a softy. She passes the time between living with her father and stepmother and living with her husband the prince in the company of seven dwarfs, who are small (as befits minor characters) and industrious. Walt Disney enlarged on this episode by giving each of the dwarfs a symbolic name: Happy, Grumpy, Doc, Sneezy, Sleepy, Bashful, and Dopey. Psychology enthusiasts would interpret these dwarfs as various representations of Snow White's identity during her transitional phase between childhood and adulthood. As an exercise in developing characters, try creating several characters who symbolize parts of your own present identity—social roles you play, or "fantasy selves" you harbor, or different aspects of your overall personality. Give each character a name. Then briefly describe each character's appearance, clothing, and home, and provide each character with a distinctive activity and cherished object. You may find yourself with a whole handful of story possibilities!

Another creativity exercise you can try is to take any list of qualities and create a character to fit each quality: for example, the seven deadly sins (pride, greed, lust, anger, gluttony, envy, and sloth) or the attributes of a good scout (trustworthy, honest, loyal, brave, kind, clean, and reverent). A reverse exercise is to think of someone you know and then think of an animal that person resembles. You don't even have to think of people you know, although they are the easiest to transpose. Try the same exercise with people you observe on the street or in a bus.

Here are some suggestions to help you build characterizations within the context of a children's story:

- *Live with your characters for a while before fitting them into the plot of a story.* Think about your characters as having their own independent existence. Imagine them in all sorts of situations: How would they behave? What would happen? Ponder your characters' backgrounds, associates, hopes, dreams, and attitudes. Only a fraction of your thoughts will eventually contribute to an individual character's role in a particular tale; but the process as a whole will help you become comfortable with him or her, learn things that will enliven your creativity and delivery, and get out of your system any extraneous details about the character that interest you but could distract attention from the main action of a specific plot. As an added bonus, you may generate material for an unending series of tales, which is less likely to happen if you initially think of the character in terms of just one story.

- *Remember that a character is best revealed through his or her actions.* In a children's story, the plot, because of its natural momentum, is more important than the characters. The characters need to emerge from the plot, rather than the plot emerging from the characters. As strong a figure as Ebenezer Scrooge is in Dickens' "A Christmas Carol," the tale as a whole is not a portrait of him but a drama about the true spirit of Christmas in which Scrooge's life is dramatized as well as the lives of the Cratchit family and Marley.

- *Concentrate on the relationships a character has, rather than on who or what the character is in isolation.* Think of your plot as a series of confrontations between the main character and other characters—confrontations that permit you and your listener to get to know the character. Eileen in "The Laziest Lass in Ireland" is immediately identified as lazy and does spend a considerable amount of time by herself; but her actual personality is exhibited through her interactions with her mother, the prince, the queen, and the three fairies.

• *Communicate a character's intentions, attitudes, opinions, wishes, and fears through his or her own voice.* Use dialogue or thinking-aloud statements to express how a character feels if the character's actions do not sufficiently or conveniently convey these feelings. Sometimes, admittedly, it is more convenient to say, "Sarasponda was sad" than to have Sarasponda sigh and say, "I'm so sad," or to have Sarasponda weeping and soaking her bright green ballgown. But bear in mind that letting a child listener actually hear Sarasponda speaking or actually see Sarasponda grieving has much more impact than bidding the child simply to take your word for how Sarasponda feels. Often you can reveal what type of personality a character has or what a character is thinking through "soft-core" action such as a character's private ritual. We see models for this in the "Mirror, mirror, on the wall" ritual of the queen in "Snow White," in the fantasy of the hero in "The Bag of Rice," and in the daydreaming of Eileen in "The Laziest Lass in Ireland."

Building an Environment

A sensitivity to the physical world in which your story takes place—the landscapes and buildings the characters inhabit, the objects they handle, the clothes they wear, the cultural trappings they exhibit—will do much to make your transmission of the tale more lively. Before you actually tell a story, map it out in your mind and walk through it with your characters, keeping all your senses open. When you are telling the story later, you will feel in some way as if you are sharing a memory. You still want to concentrate on actions in your story, and not on descriptions; but some degree of description is essential and desirable. The challenge is to keep this description crisp and relevant to the plot.

Suppose your story takes place in a real city, like Paris. A child may have no concept of Paris at all, so you will want to provide that child with some sort of clear image. If your hero is a young, callow lad out to seek his fortune, you could work in a reference to Paris as a city "full of marketplaces where money is exchanged, full of statues erected to people who accomplished great deeds, and full of restaurants where rich people eat strange foods like snails and frogs." If your story takes place in an imaginary kingdom, you can invent one or two distinctive characteristics of the people, or the way they live, or the countryside. Depending on the nature of the plot, maybe it is a place where "everyone works hard to make a living" or a place where "everyone sleeps with a nightcap."

The best way to communicate the environment of a story is through the actions in a story. Have your characters perform tasks that fit their situations, employing relevant tools and gadgets. Use words that are especially evocative of the cultural climate or physical conditions that exist in the realm of your story. Take, for example, the case of a young girl who journeys from her cottage to the home of her uncle. According to the general locale of your story, you can have her crossing glens and bogs, or forests of pine and meadows of wildflowers, or prairies and wheatfields. You don't have to describe these features; your colorful selection of words to identify them is enough. Children delight in hearing fresh, well-chosen terms.

Perhaps a story's environment is quite unique and a central element of your story idea. The action could occur in Toyland or Oz or Upsidedownia. I particularly liked Al Capp's Upper Slobbovia when I was a child—a country forever blanketed in snow and ice that was modeled on popular fantasies of Siberia. I was also fascinated by Bizarro, a parallel world featured occasionally in *Superman* comics where everything is slightly off kilter. Carl Sandburg's *Rootabaga Tales* contains many spectacular illustrations of make-believe realms. In creating a deliberately strange environment, you will need to work out in advance a limited number of particularly interesting features that can be illustrated through the plot.

Many of the most endearing children's stories are ones that take place in a closed environment—on an island, in a small village, in the attic of a mansion, or, in Peter Rabbit's case, in a backyard garden. I once worked in a bookmobile that made regular storytelling stops. Inspired by the bus filled up with kids, I would tell stories about Captain Mucilage's seafaring ventures with his crew, the Modern Library Giants, on the miraculously well-equipped ship, *Checkout*. I had to do research every now and then concerning the parts of a ship, the roles played by different members of a ship's crew, and the jargon used by mariners; but the research was fun and resulted in lots of new story ideas.

You may want to investigate a specific closed world that interests you. It may be based on your job, in which case you can indirectly communicate to a child the type of world where you yourself spend a great deal of time. Or it may be based on a vacation spot or a local cave complex or an imposing house in your neighborhood.

Physical objects are also part of a tale's environment. A character can be closely associated with a special talisman or totem that is, among other things, symbolic of the overall physical setting of the story. Among well-known children's stories, such items include the handhewn hickory stick of Johnny Appleseed; the cherished gold doubloon of Pluck, the young explorer in "The Knight of Wonders"; and the elaborately decorated shield of Achilles. Consider unusual objects in your own surroundings: Maybe you can create a whole story to explain them.

Relating Real-Life Adventure Stories

Many people are not comfortable recounting real-life adventure stories, especially when those stories are basically about friends, relatives, or themselves. Either they don't remember any such tales clearly or they're inhibited by trying to speak "nothing but the truth."

A real-life adventure story is primarily like any other story. You do want to preserve the same fundamental story idea, characters, events, and environment each time you tell a real-life adventure story, so you have somewhat less freedom when it comes to adaptation. But you remain free to embroider, exaggerate, and invent details that better dramatize the meaning of the story.

There are as many perspectives on any real-life adventure story as there are witnesses to that story. If the story is about something you experienced, you know that the experience was full of a great deal of personal drama that may not be apparent if you simply recite the bald details of what occurred. Give the story an equivalent sense of drama when you tell it to a listener. Your listener knows it's storytelling time. Children earnestly and carefully construct lots of stories about themselves expressly designed to communicate the "truth" of a particular event as opposed to the mere factual content of a particular event.

When you create a real-life adventure story, think of what you want to say and what your listener wants to hear. Where these two meet is where your story lies.

The problem of remembering real-life stories is a tricky one.

Fictitious stories have special hooks in them to ensure that they will be retained. Real-life adventure stories often lack neat beginnings and endings.

Try reading biographies and autobiographies of people who interest you. Ask your friends and relatives to tell you stories they know. As for stories from your own life, make a list of events that are clear and vivid in your memory: funny episodes, or educational ones, or inspirational ones. Maybe they were turning points; perhaps, instead, they were "sideline" incidents. Ask yourself which ones involved another family member as well. Maybe you can ask that person to restimulate your memory. Certainly you can involve that relative as a major character in your story. Then ask yourself which ones involve a child. Children are vitally interested in stories about themselves or other children. Finally, ask yourself what connections you can draw among these events. Do any share a common theme? It may start you on the way to collecting individual scenes for an overall story.

In one respect, you have more freedom telling real-life adventure stories about yourself than you do telling any other type of tale. Your story can be more loosely crafted and can include more description. Because the listener is hearing the story "from the horse's mouth," he or she is bound to be more curious about, even eager for, details and won't be concerned if your story lacks a tight narrative structure. Here is an example from *A Celebration of American Folklore* contributed by Sharon Baber of Arlington, Virginia, that illustrates how appealing such a story can be, despite the fact that it is long on description and short on structure.

When I was growing up in St. Louis during World War II, the kids in the neighborhood would get together and go en masse to the neighborhood theater. We'd have our ten cents to get in and our five cents for popcorn, and we'd go, six or eight or ten or twelve of us, at ten in the morning and stay until six at night. During the war, there was such a shortage of gasoline, rubber and metal. One way to encourage people to get scrap metal was to have kids bring it to the movies on Saturday. We'd each have to bring a piece of metal and that was our entrance fee. If you didn't have your piece of metal, you would have to pay a dime to get in. The metal would be piled up in a parking lot and then they would send it down to be melted down for airplanes and whatever else was needed. I once donated my pair of roller skates and then I cried afterwards, wishing I still had them. A couple of kids took their mothers' good pots and pans from the kitchen and some took their fathers' tools out of the tool chest . . . anything to get metal so that we could get into the movies.

Consider also telling stories solely about your listener. One father I know discovered that among his three-year-old child's favorite bedtime stories was a recapitulation of her own day. A typical story would begin: "Once upon a time there was a beautiful girl named Judy. She woke up in the morning and stretched and jumped out of bed . . ."

Creative Variations on Storytelling

The best creative stories are the ones we fashion ourselves, from beginning to end. But we inevitably wind up using elements that relate to other stories we have read or heard. You may want to experiment with borrowing plot structures, specific scenes, characters, or an environment from a story you like. Maybe you will want to compose a tale about what happened before, or after, the time span of a well-known story.

Rereading favorite stories can also trigger altogether new story ideas. A good friend of mine, Tom Cowan, the author of several works on intuition, has always been struck by the words of Ben Gunn in Robert Louis Stevenson's *Treasure Island* when Gunn has his first conversation with a human being after being marooned for three years: ". . . many's the long night I've dreamed of cheese." Think of the many story ideas that could be sparked merely by playing around with substitutions for the word "cheese"!

When you create your own stories, consider the possibility of developing a continuing saga. The same character or characters can appear in any number of different stories. Or different characters can appear in the same environment in different stories. One of my favorite plot models for a continuing saga is the story structure of Antoine de Saint-Exupery's *The Little Prince*—featuring a tiny space wanderer who visits one tiny planet after another, each planet having a particular type of eccentric inhabitant. When I was in grade school, I used to make up stories for my friends and relatives about a mouse named El Squeako—a combination of the popular television characters Mighty Mouse and Zorro. El Squeako traveled far and wide in different stories, usually by ship, naturally. I also made up stories about a village called "Insomnia," each story highlighting a different act of stupidity by a different village citizen.

Joe Carson, a professor of language and literature at Shelby State Community College in Memphis, Tennessee, invented a stock set of characters for an ongoing series of stories he told to his twin daughters, Jennifer and Emily, who are my godchildren. "It was my apple family," he explains. "Jonathan, the handsome oldest brother; York, the squat and comical younger brother who became a football player; Red Delicious, or Red D., the youngest and wildest, the redhead who was close to the one sister, Apple Blossom, or Apple B. The parents died in the first episode, which I modeled on a *Little House on the Prairie* show I had seen with Jennifer and Emily. Indeed, *Little House* remained the main source outside my head."

Another variation on storytelling that can be an enormous amount of fun for you and your listener is participatory storytelling, where you begin a story and stop at a highly dramatic point, asking your listener to continue the story for a while. You can go back and forth this way, weaving any type of wild story you wish: The exchange is the important thing here. Because it is such a loose version of storytelling, do not expect the finished product, in itself, to be all that satisfying. Use participatory storytelling sparingly. Save it for moments when you and your listener both feel in the mood for it. From my own experience, I offer one note of caution: Think ahead of time how you will reply if, after having brought your hero to a crisis point, your listener takes over and says, ". . . and then he dropped dead."

The more you get involved in creating your own stories, the more variations on storytelling you will discover. There are a thousand variations, in the Arabic sense of the term "thousand," which is to say, they are limitless in number. Every time you communicate, new possibilities for storytelling variations open up. In becoming a teller of original tales, you are preparing yourself to recognize and exploit these possibilities.

Pathways To Storytelling

• Set a goal for yourself to create a story for a special occasion: a listener's birthday, a holiday, or a visit to a new and exciting place.

• Write descriptions of people you know pretty well. Experiment with different types of descriptions; for example, ones that show that person's virtues and ones that show that person's faults. Note the words and incidents in each case that seem to be the most effective in communicating your intention. They will be helpful to you in developing characters and plots for stories.

• Write a paragraph that describes a room, a building, or a place you remember vividly from your childhood. Note the words that seem particularly successful in communicating a child's point of view. They will

be helpful to you in developing environments for stories.

• Keep a log of words that strike you as unusually interesting, humorous, dramatic, or melodic. You can work them into stories for special effect.

• Clip news articles that describe strange objects, or customs, or ways of life. Pay close attention to classified ads that outline unusual job opportunities or professions and to personal ads that characterize people and their desires in imaginative ways. These items can inspire a number of entertaining stories.

• Experiment with enlisting another person to help you create a story—someone who is clever at spinning yarns or sharing anecdotes, or someone who knows your listener well.

CHAPTER SIX

TELLING STORIES

Friends and relatives have often said to me, "I wish I could write a book." In many cases, the remark saddens me, because the people who make it are people who tell wonderful stories all the time. They simply don't realize that telling stories is as creative and important as writing stories. They fail to take telling stories seriously.

One reason may be that anyone can tell stories, once he or she learns a language. Some people seem to do it better than others, and so we tend to think they are naturally gifted storytellers or that special circumstances have transformed them into unusually good storytellers.

The ability to spin an enjoyable tale is not a genetic trait that manifests itself among people who are close to the soil, or put lampshades on their heads at parties, or while away their hours reading, or hang around taverns on weeknights. Nor do you need to have crossed Greenland on foot to have stories to tell. You already possess all the abilities and materials you need to tell stories. The charm that will turn you into a storyteller is the conscious decision to take those abilities and materials seriously. Then you will tell stories more easily and successfully, without inhibitions. You will also be more inclined to practice your skills and prepare for applying them, which is the only way anyone becomes a better storyteller.

Choosing a Good Time

As a child I marveled at what I believed was my grandmother's unique talent for picking just the right moment to tell a story. Whenever I felt I needed her gift of total attention to me, sometimes even before I knew I wanted it, there she would be, saying, "Once, very far away and long ago . . ." I thought it was part of the same magic that lay in her shinbones and warned her when it would rain. "Irish blood," I said to myself.

When I was in graduate school in Boston, I drove a cab at night and frequently passed through her neighborhood. Many times I would drop in to see her and to collect family-history stories. I asked her on one of these visits how she had known when I, my brother, or my cousins wanted to hear a story. She seemed surprised. "It was nothing at all," she insisted. "I never thought about it. It's not hard to spot when a child is run out and ready for a story—not if you've been waiting all day for it!"

I was not entirely satisfied with my grandmother's answer. At the time, rationalist and fledgling adult that I was, I believed there must be a secret technique. But my own experiences with children have confirmed that one doesn't need a sixth sense to choose the right time for storytelling.

Whenever you feel you would like to tell a story and a child is close at hand, a potentially wonderful storytelling opportunity exists. And it is in your power, native bard or not, to make the most of such opportunities—first, by ensuring that they arise with predictable frequency and, second, by preparing yourself so that when the time comes, you can set the right tone and deliver a story skillfully, as if by second nature.

The most advantageous circumstance for storytelling is in the context of a regularly scheduled daily story time, one you and your listener can look forward to with pleasure. When storytelling is an organic part of each day, both of you will participate in it more naturally, with more cooperation and more mental and emotional absorption.

All children, from infancy through the teenage years, enjoy rituals. They provide a much-needed sense of security in a world that is frequently baffling and full of unwelcome surprises. And the ritual can begin as soon as the child is born. The steady bond that it will develop between the two of you can form a solid foundation for future sessions, when the child is more capable of understanding the situations and feelings the stories convey. Eventually these memories will help a child to read alone.

Once a child is six or seven years old and has begun reading alone fairly competently, the benefits of storytelling are even greater. Then it can breathe life into the child's own experience with language and point the way to further reading, as well as provide assurance that you are remaining in touch—that your intimacy has not ceased now that the child is more independent. The pleasure and value of this kind of communion can continue for the child the rest of his or her life.

The exact time and duration of a regularly scheduled storytelling session need to be flexible to fit the day itself. But after you have experimented and discovered which part of the day works best for you and your listener, try to stick to it. This will give structure to the session and make it easier to manage. Preferably, you will select a time when you and your listener will be free from distractions and interruptions.

Bedtime is perhaps the most congenial time for storytelling. All of us, children most especially, seek a spiritual balance at the end of the day, before yielding to sleep. Even the child who is most reluctant to go to bed will be eager to do so if it means enjoying a story. And the story itself will have a calming influence, directing the listener inward and away from the demands and counterdemands of the real world.

For two- to four-year-olds, bedtime storytelling can operate as a uniquely effective therapeutic aid. According to psychiatrist Selma Freiberg, "It is distressing to the child who has newly found his or her identity to see it disappear as consciousness dissolves in the moments before falling asleep." Storytelling can function as a bridge between consciousness and unconsciousness, allowing the child to disengage comfortably from self-importance and enter a state of dreamlike surrender.

If your listener has little trouble going to bed at night but resists interrupting the day to rest, you may want to set up a regularly scheduled storytelling session just before naptime (the acronym of probably the most vigorous American storytelling organization, the

National Association for the Preservation and Perpetuation of Storytelling, NAPPS, always makes me think of this). If nothing else, listening to a story gets a child's mind off the notion of resisting a nap.

Storytelling can also console and restore a child who is apprehensive about leaving home for school each day. Sharing this moment with you convinces the child of your love and support and, most significantly, of his or her own personal worthiness—precisely when it is about to be challenged by other children vying for teacher and peer recognition.

At school, knowing that a specific time is slated for daily storytelling can make a child more willing to expend his or her mental energies during the basic instructional class periods. The process of relaxing and listening to a story also allows students to let their minds wander over what they have learned. They can consciously or unconsciously associate details in a story with some of their thoughts, which will make those thoughts easier to remember later.

Storytelling is an irreplaceable means for a teacher to become a more effective role model for his or her students. A teacher telling a story is living proof of the positive results of reading widely and developing one's powers of imagination. Because of the inspirational effect such modeling can have on a student, storytelling well deserves a fixed time of its own on the schoolday's agenda.

Whether or not storytelling can be regularly scheduled, it works most successfully at those moments when you want to create a change of pace or when a change of pace occurs naturally. "Storytelling is a very precious, very powerful force," cautions Mark Mintner, who supervises a day-care center in Los Angeles. "It should not be thrown in front of children like a toy, or it will be wasted. I wait for the end of an activity or for those times when there aren't a lot of competing interests."

If you are a teacher, you may want to slot storytelling between two very diverse activities as a way of refreshing your students and helping them to be ready for new experiences. An ideal time would be between an intellectually taxing lesson and a more open-ended activity, such as drawing, dancing, or recess.

If you are a special guest and have only a short time to be with a child, it is probably best to reserve storytelling until just before you leave, after the child has had a chance to become accustomed to your presence. These few minutes together will ease the separation for the child and leave him or her with a warm memory of your visit. Repeated contacts can follow the same pattern, endowing your relationship with a colorful character all its own.

Storytelling does not have to be a dependable or routine event to cast its magic. It makes an excellent unexpected treat, provided both you and your listener are in the mood. If you spend large amounts of time around a child, trust daily life to present you with numerous opportunities for spontaneous storytelling: in a car during a traffic jam, while waiting in a dentist's office, when a longed-for baseball game is rained out—anytime when you and a child find yourselves marooned together. Special occasions during the year seem to beg for storytelling: yarns of faraway places in the course of a long plane trip, tales of ancient traditions and celebrations after a holiday meal, ghost stories around a campfire on a fall weekend.

Crises constantly threaten to engulf children: A favorite toy breaks, a dreaded confrontation looms, an anxiously awaited letter does not arrive. When things go wrong, storytelling can be a wonderfully personal way of easing a child's pain and reaffirming his or her faith in life. It doesn't matter if the tale itself corresponds in some fashion to the situation of the child. In fact, it may be better if you don't try to effect a correspondence, since it can make your listener self-conscious. What is meaningful is the event itself, which transcends its content.

When I was a counselor at a summer camp in southern Ohio, one of my campers was an overweight, bespectacled, and very clever nine-year-old named Brian. I watched him unobserved one after-noon as he squirmed in a line of boys being chosen for either the Dolphin or the Shark swim relay teams by the respective team captains. Sure in his heart that he would be the last one picked, Brian calculated which team would be stuck with him and wandered over to it ahead of time, probably hoping to win some appreciative laughs to cushion the embarrassment. Instead, he was matter-of-factly advised that he did not have to stick around—the first-chosen swimmer would perform two rounds. Brian's face sank.

As Brian stumbled away through the woods toward our cabin, I followed him and maneuvered an accidental meeting. I said that I, too, was on my way back for a rest and asked him if he would like me to tell him about Jason and the Argonauts. He nodded weakly and slumped along beside me, still dazed by his recent humiliation. But as I told the story of the quest for the golden fleece, his eyes began to light up again and he rocked with excitement. Later he repeated the story for other campers, including some Sharks and Dolphins, and his enthusiasm was spellbinding.

It is not difficult to choose a good time for storytelling if you respect what it offers: a quiet and strong moment of communion. Both you and your listener need to be open to sharing. Storytelling is not a means of offering a sermon or a lesson in disguise. It loses its value and beauty when it is bartered as a sop to a child who is throwing a tantrum, or as a reward for a mischievous child's good behavior, or as one of a number of entertainment options to beguile a child who is bored.

Telling a story is offering an expression of love. It derives its meaning not so much from what is said as from how it is said. For this reason, experienced storytellers devote some of their attention to orchestrating the storytelling session as a whole, so that it stands the best chance of being pleasurable for both the teller and the listener.

Creating a Positive Environment

The key to establishing the right atmosphere for storytelling is to be confident of your command of the story and of the story's merits. If you have this confidence, you will be able to tell stories naturally and easily, without histrionics and strain but with an apparent simplicity that will comfort the listener.

Storytelling is undeniably dramatic in nature, but it does not require all the techniques and discipline of acting, oral interpretation, or even recitation. It is a self-contained narrative performance, with its own nutrients for both the listener and the teller. Your aim as the teller is not to identify with the characters in the story but to communicate the overall feeling of the story. The essence of storytelling, its gestalt, is giving expression to what moves you—finding your voice and using it to share a tale that means something special to you.

Before beginning the session, concentrate on what that special meaning is for each of the stories you plan to offer. Does the Norwegian folktale "East of the Sun and West of the Moon" appeal to you because of the repentant character of the princess who searches desperately for the prince she wronged, or because of the spectacular nature of her journey: the long high ride on the back of the North Wind and the miraculous land of mirrors? When you think of "Paul Bunyan and Babe the Blue Ox," do you appreciate most the heartiness of the logging community or the solitary splendor of the childlike giant and his beloved companion?

You may want to meditate on this meaning prior to conducting a storytelling session, even if it's only for a few moments. This is also a good method for overcoming any stage fright you may have and for adding a peaceful intensity to your eventual delivery. It is a matter of putting yourself in the mood to tell a story (and to rehear it yourself) rather than of testing yourself to see if you remember the story.

If you are completely absorbed in what you are doing, it will go smoothly. This is true of everything from cooking lasagna or doing knee bends to being a productive employee or a caring partner. One way of attaining this degree of absorption in the story you are sharing is to visualize each scene as you are telling it. While you speak of Hansel and Gretel wandering through the forest, uncertain of where they are, imagine the thorny bramblebushes and the thick gnarled oaks catching the last golden glints of the setting sun. When you begin the tale of Sir Gawain and the Green Knight, see the heavy doors bang open into the crowded, brightly lit banquet hall and watch the torch flames flicker as the hideous intruder strides forward to challenge the valiant knights of the Round Table.

If this kind of visualization comes easily to you, you may prefer the even more imaginative approach suggested by one of the most famous American professional storytellers, Eulalie Steinmetz Ross:

> Bring to the telling of the story any experience, any memory, any knowledge from life that will give breadth and depth to its interpretation. Hear the "Sleeping Beauty Waltz" as the French fairy tale weaves its spell of enchantment. See the Chicago skyline as the background for Carl Sandburg's "Two Skyscrapers Who Decided to Have a Child." Remember the last line of Robert Frost's poem, "Stopping by the Woods on a Snowy Evening" as you tell Mary Wilkin's "The Silver Hen."

As you train yourself to feel the events of the story while you are relating them, you unconsciously guide your listener to do the same. Your tempo will match the logical pace of the story, and your language will be convincing and appropriately stimulating to the senses. It is in this manner that storytelling becomes not only easy but an adventure.

A well-controlled storytelling session encourages a child to listen with deep quietness. Before you start, be sure that you and your listener are comfortable and facing each other. Maintaining eye contact throughout the storytelling session accomplishes four purposes: It helps you to concentrate; it increases your listener's attentiveness; it enables you to gauge your listener's responses; and, most importantly, it adds to the intimacy of the occasion. Break eye contact only to look at an imaginary scene or object that you especially want your listener to envision or, if you wish, to mimic characters who are conversing with each other. You can communicate a great deal with your eyes; but you may want to take advantage of logical moments for breaking eye contact in order to prevent yourself from merely staring at your listener.

Beginnings

Depending on the circumstances, you may want to open a storytelling session with a simple ceremony to reinforce the impression that this is a special event. Traditionally, storytelling hours in American libraries feature a "wishing candle," lit at the beginning of the session and extinguished at the end. It's a simple gesture that evokes celebration, dreams, magic, and the past. At bedtime it may even wean a child from insisting on sleeping with a light burning. You can say, "The story will sound much better if I turn off the lamp." Subdued lighting, however achieved, will bring you and your listener much closer to each other.

Another effective device is to use a fanciful gimmick for summoning the story itself. Pretend to pull a story hat from your listener's ear and put it on your head, or pantomime listening to an elf who is standing on tiptoe beside you to whisper suggestions. Alice Toley, a librarian in Manhattan, verbally invites the story to come, in a manner that subtly works to make the audience even more attentive: "Now that our sound is the sound of clouds moving, or berries reddening, or the moon shining, which is to say, no sound at all, let the story come and be spoken."

Professional storytellers down through the ages have often employed little game devices to get their listeners to commit themselves to a listening mode. Such devices feature a call-and-response exchange between the teller and the listener. In Haiti, when a teller wants to find out if anyone desires to listen to his or her tale, he or she shouts, "Cric?" If someone is interested, he or she responds, "Crac!" Among the Mohawk Indians, the teller says, "Ho?" and the consenting listener answers, "Hey!" Exchanging your own private storytelling passwords with a listener is a quick and easy way of settling down to business.

How you start the storytelling session can have a lot to do with the age of your audience. Children around nine to twelve years old, for example, are beginning to study social sciences and to develop an interest in history and biography, prompted by a dawning curiosity about their own personality growth. They may appreciate knowing the actual source or background of a story. A few words about the context of the story—how you first encountered it, who created it, explanations of unusual customs or objects in the tale— may be an appropriate preface for this age group. Be careful, however, not to delve into the meaning of the story in any way, as this will prejudice the free response of the listener.

Beginning the story itself with a formulaic phrase, such as "Once upon a time . . ." has been a popular device throughout recorded history in all parts of the world, regardless of the age of the listener. There is a very good reason for this: It sets the make-believe world of a story firmly apart from the real world. This particular opening is now so closely associated with storytelling that it serves as an almost subliminal cue for both teller and listener to slip into a receptive frame of mind. You do not have to begin, literally, with "Once upon a time . . ." There are endless variations: some referring to special places, like "In a magic kingdom far beyond the farthest place an eagle can fly . . .," or special conditions, like "In a time when wishes still had power . . ."

You can invent your own trademark expression or switch openings according to the nature of the session or the story. Several years ago, telling a Shoshoni Indian fable to a couple of children in Ketchum, Idaho, I was able to say, "Once, back in the time of your father's father's father's father's father, on this very spot, before there was any road or house or even clear land, there lived an Indian boy named Blue Fox."

Interruptions

Is it true?

Most often you can answer this by saying something like, "This is a make-believe truth. In stories, many things are true that aren't exactly true in real life." According to J. R. R. Tolkien, the actual concern of the listener is likely to be " 'Was he good? Was he wicked?' That is, [the child] is more concerned to get the Right side and the Wrong side clear." Tolkien also discusses another possible concern behind the question: "Often enough what children mean when they ask: 'Is it true?' [is] 'I like this, but is it contemporary? Am I safe in my bed?' The answer: 'There is certainly no dragon in England today' is all that they want to hear." If you are uncertain what the child is asking, pose an open-ended question of your own to clarify the situation.

What does that mean?

Any question from your listener about the meaning of a word or about a person, place, activity, or thing mentioned in your story needs to be answered very briefly and conclusively at the time it is raised. Try to maintain the same overall tone you are using to tell the story in your response. If you can, provide a natural transition between your explanation and the next moment in the story.

I'm scared!

Acknowledge that what you have said is, indeed, scary and immediately introduce something to alleviate that feeling— the sudden occurrence of a solution or the sudden appearance of a rescuer. Consider bringing the story quickly to a positive end and offering a short, upbeat story to conclude the storytelling session.

I don't like this story.

You can stop right away and say, "Well, we will save it for a better time." Depending on your sense of the circumstances, you can ask your listener if he or she would like to hear another story or do something else. If the child wants to continue the storytelling session itself, switch to an entirely different type of story, preferably a shorter one. This could be a good time to try a storytelling poem, song, or game instead. If you avoid taking the remark personally and simply end the session gently, there is no harm done.

I have to go to the bathroom.

Similar kinds of remarks are, "I want a glass of water" or "Where's my black rabbit?" Again, you need to consider the general circumstances, asking open-ended questions of your listener if you are not sure what to do. You have a number of options. You can allow the interruption to run its course and return as soon as possible to the story, or you can stop the story, saying you will tell it again some other time, or you can quickly bring the story to a conclusion. The same procedure applies to any outside interruption you cannot put aside. Say something, in any case, to create an easy and quick break from the story itself.

Middles

Speak as you would normally speak when you are telling a story. You can trust the dramatic nature of the story to have an immediate effect on how you tell it. You don't need to make a conscious effort to speak dramatically, because you are not performing. You are communicating.

Here are some guidelines you can follow if you want to work on improving your ability to deliver stories effectively:

- *Speak in low, modulated tones.* The most common fault of storytellers is that they assume an artificial, uncomfortable voice when they are telling their tales. In most cases, this makes the voice too high and thin, causing the teller to speak too rapidly all through the story. If you speak in your usual "low" voice, your sound is richer, your pace is more measured, and your enunciation is more distinct. Avoid baby talk or talking down to your listener. Avoid hemming and hawing, punctuating pauses with "uh's," "er's," "and's," or "you see's." If you need to stop and think, stop gently and be still. Take a breath. Keep eye contact. Resume gently.

- *Vary the rhythm of your delivery.* Poetic, imaginative, or descriptive passages are best spoken slowly, so that the listener can get a full picture of something new. (One reason why I advise against including long descriptive passages in a story is that such passages do slow the story down a bit.) Whenever we talk about actions, we tend to speak more rapidly; talking about actions in stories is no exception. Let the action passages be quick and spirited. When you are speaking as one of the characters, use a speed and a rhythm appropriate to that character. You can shade the way the character speaks so that he or she has a somewhat different voice, but don't overdo it. Pretend you are telling your listener what a friend of yours said. Make any variations you may wish among characters' voices in terms of whether an individual voice is low or high, loud or soft, fast or slow. A dropped voice is frequently more effective than a raised voice when you are communicating something dramatic about a person, place, or thing. When events are urgent, speak of them with urgency. Build to the climax of a story by speeding up near the end; and when you reach the end, let your voice fall away gradually.

- *Use pauses for special effect.* The pause is more powerful than any other single speaking device in lending a story drama and energy. The more you practice pausing at appropriate times, the more you will be convinced of this. It allows space for what you have said to resonate and for events, moods, and tones to shift smoothly. It offers you a chance to absorb some of the pleasure you have been generating and to share a silent moment of wonder with your storytelling partner. It also gives you time to breathe. Pause before a change of idea, before a significant word, before saying who it is who suddenly appears, before speaking the actual reply a character makes to a dramatic question.

- *Be flexible with your vocabulary.* Don't worry about whether a particular word you wish to use will be too obscure for your listener. Don't break the pace of your story to consider, How shall I put this? You may want to prepare yourself ahead of time to be a more lively storyteller in general by thinking up synonyms for some of the more commonly used words in stories, such as "beautiful," "ugly," "large," "small," "house," "think," "walk," and "say." You may want to give some of your characters special terms they alone use—odd words or nonsense exclamations or unusual oaths. Choose or invent terms that sound like what they describe: A character can, for example, "garrumph" instead of "exclaim"; a cat can "tap" rather than "walk" across a room. You can also make words sound more appropriate by emphasizing vowels: for example, saying "*soooo huuuuge*" when you are referring to a vast chamber.

- *Allow gestures to come naturally.* Elocutionists around the turn of the century were fond of employing exaggerated gestures to accompany the mood or content of what they were saying. We can still see the effects of this style in silent films (where, admittedly, something had to be done in the absence of sound) and in the talent routines of losing contenders for the Miss America title. It is wise not to make a special effort to insert gestures into your delivery of a story. It could keep you from relaxing while you are telling it. If a gesture is clumsy, it can distract attention from the content of what you are saying or expose the story as a contrived performance piece. Gestures that arise naturally and spontaneously as you tell a story can be very effective in captivating your listener—particularly facial gestures and hand movements. Like pauses, they can add drama and emphasis to key points in a story. Gestures are especially successful when they help to define a character's personality, or when they serve to make a complicated physical piece of business (such as spinning and weaving in "The Laziest Lass in Ireland") more tangible, or when they assist a listener to envision a distinctive type of building, landscape, or object. Make sure any gesture you use comes at the same time, or slightly before, the words you are trying to illustrate or empha- size. A gesture that comes later causes your pace to falter and may contradict the mental picture your listener has already formed.

- *Relax, breathe easily, and feel your voice.* One of the great pleasures storytelling offers for the teller is the opportunity to experience his or her own voice when it is liable to be at its richest. While you are telling a story, keep one ear cocked to your own sound. Most likely this will not only help you speak in a rhythm that moves in harmony with your breathing, but it will also encourage you to breathe more deeply and speak from the diaphragm—the manner of vocalizing that produces the most well rounded tones. The sensation you get when you do this is quite soothing and motivates you to deliver a story even more confidently and effectively. If you wish to practice dia- phragm breathing, so that you can feel your voice all across your chest and not just in your throat, you may want to try an exercise designed by Ruth Sawyer, a highly popular American storyteller throughout the first half of this century:

> Learn to control the breath by the abdominal muscles, not the throat muscles. If you are not sure what you do, find out—it is very easy. Speak a few sentences aloud with a hand cupped not too tightly around your throat. If you feel no constriction, nothing but the epiglottis moving slightly up and down, your throat is free from constriction. If you can feel a tightening of any muscle in the throat, no matter how slight it may be, you are not speaking freely or correctly. . . . Now then: first put your hands above your hips,

thumbs to the back. Expel breath with all the positive force you can muster through an open mouth; press in your hands as hard as you can. You are externally making your diaphragm muscles contract. You should be making them contract under their own power. Draw in the breath slowly, through nose and mouth, letting your hands relax and getting the feeling of your muscles taking hold. Repeat this until you begin to feel breath riding upon those muscles. Concentration, the will to try it over and over, does it.

It is not essential that you practice improving your breathing in order to tell a story well; but the ability to breathe correctly does far more than improve your health and the sound of your speaking voice. It focuses your energy and makes you calmer. It also gives you more control over the emotional content of what you say.

Endings

Formulaic endings to a story are as important as formulaic beginnings. They return the listener smoothly and efficiently to the everyday world and help the teller to end the story with a minimum of fuss.

You will find that the expression ". . . and they lived happily ever after" will not fit every story. Many popular storytellers employ a signature phrase, such as Ruth Sawyer's "Take this story and may the next one who tells it make it better" or Ted Michaelis' ". . . and so it goes and continues to go whenever a listener wishes to know." The majority of children's stories you hear or read will have their own built-in endings or will provide you with clues for inventing appropriate endings.

How you end the storytelling session as a whole may depend on how you began it. If you lit a wishing candle, then you need to blow it out. If you caught the story in the air, then you have to toss it back. If you don't have any special ceremony to perform, be sure to make a distinct break between the storytelling session and your next words to a child. Let a pause occur or change your tone. If you are telling a story at bedtime and your listener appears to have fallen asleep during the story, bring it to an end anyway and then say a separate "good night." Your listener may only be experiencing what is known as a "hypnagogic state," still subconsciously attuned to what you are saying.

It is best not to ask your listener to comment on the story or to indicate whether he or she enjoyed it. Leave the story and the telling of it to work their own spells for a while.

The Living Story

In order to give you a sense of how a particular story may be effectively delivered using some of the suggestions offered in this chapter, I would like to walk you through a short adapted version of a tale entitled "The Six Sillies," which appears in Andrew Lang's *The Red Fairy Book*. I have choreographed the tale so that each individual recommendation for the storyteller appears on the right side of the page directly across, where possible, from the passage to which it relates. These recommendations in no way reflect the way the story has to be told in order for it to be successful. They are only possibilities to consider. Anyone else choreographing this story may come up with different, equally good suggestions.

THE THREE SILLIES

Once upon a time there was a young woman who wanted to get married; but she was so silly, no one wanted to marry her. One day there was a knock at the door, and her mother jumped up from her knitting to answer it. She opened the door, and there, in front of her, was a handsome young man who said, "I've come to court your daughter." The mother, beaming with joy, sent her daughter down to the cellar to draw a jug of ale.

EMPHASIZE "SILLY."

PAUSE SLIGHTLY AFTER "THERE" AND "HER."

Since her daughter didn't come back, the mother went down to see what had happened to her and found her sitting on the stairs, with her head in her hands, while beside her the ale was running all over the floor, because she had forgotten to turn off the tap. "What are you doing here?" asked the mother. "I was wondering what I shall call my first child after I am married to the young man," said the woman. "All the names in the calendar are already taken." The mother sat down beside her daughter and said, "I will think about it with you, my dear."

PAUSE SLIGHTLY AFTER
". . . HAPPENED TO HER."

SAY "ALL OVER THE
FLOOR" SLOWLY.

MOTHER SPEAKS WITH
QUIET WONDER.

DAUGHTER RESPONDS
ALMOST CASUALLY,
WITHOUT SADNESS. SHE
IS ONLY A BIT
EXASPERATED.

MOTHER SPEAKS WITH
SOME JOY. SHE IS A HAPPY
PERSON AND SHE IS
SETTLING DOWN TO
HELP HER DAUGHTER.

The father, who had stayed upstairs with the young man, wondered why his wife and daughter were not returning, so he came down and found them both sitting on the stairs, while beside them the ale was running all over the floor. "What are you doing here?" he asked. "We were thinking what we should call the first child that our daughter will have after she marries the young man," the mother answered. "All the names in the calendar

SAY "ALL OVER THE
FLOOR" SLOWLY.

FATHER SPEAKS WITH
SOME DEGREE OF
IRRITATION,
EMPHASIZING "ARE."
MOTHER ANSWERS
CONFIDENTLY, AS IF SHE
HAS A GOOD ANSWER.

are already taken." "Ah, well, I will think about it with you," said the father.

SAY "AH, WELL" SLOWLY. FATHER IS COMING AROUND TO MOTHER'S POINT OF VIEW.

At last, the lover grew impatient waiting all alone and went down himself to see what they could all be doing. He found all three of them sitting on the stairs while beside them the ale was running all over the floor. "What in the world are you all doing that you don't come upstairs and that you let the ale run all over the floor?" he asked. "Oh, my young man," said the father, "we were wondering. What shall you call your first child? All the names in the calendar are taken."

SAY "ALL OVER THE FLOOR" SLOWLY. LOVER SPEAKS LOUD AND FAST. HE IS JUSTIFIED IN HIS ANGER BUT ALMOST COMICAL IN THE WAY HE EXPRESSES IT. MAYBE GESTURE TO GO WITH "DOING," "COME UPSTAIRS," AND "LET THE ALE RUN."

FATHER SPEAKS POLITELY AND FORMALLY.

The young man stared at them with amazement. "Well that does it!" he exclaimed. "I'm going away. When I have found three people sillier than you I will come back and marry your daughter."

SPEAK SLOWLY. EMPHASIZE "STARED AT." AND "AMAZEMENT." PAUSE SLIGHTLY AFTER "AMAZEMENT." LOVER SPEAKS FIRMLY.

EMPHASIZE "SILLIER."

So the young man stormed out and wandered across the farmlands until he reached an orchard. He stopped

SPEAK THE FIRST SENTENCE RAPIDLY.

SPEAK THE SECOND SENTENCE SLOWLY.

suddenly when he saw a laborer knocking down walnuts and trying to throw them into a cart with a fork. "What are you doing there?" he asked. "I want to take my walnuts to the market," said the laborer, "but I can't seem to get them into my cart very easily." "Get a basket," the lover advised. "Then put the walnuts into the basket and empty it into the cart." "How very clever you are," said the laborer, went off for a basket. "My stars!" said the lover to himself. "I have already found someone more foolish than those three!"

LOVER SPEAKS ABRUPTLY IN THIS EPISODE.

LABORER SPEAKS NATURALLY. THE LISTENER NEEDS TO HEAR THIS CLEARLY AND YOU DO NOT WANT TO GIVE THIS MINOR CHARACTER (OR OTHERS) TOO STRONG A PERSONALITY.

EMPHASIZE "GET."

EMPHASIZE "PUT."

EMPHASIZE "EMPTY."

PAUSE AFTER "BASKET."
EMPHASIZE "MY STARS!"

So he continued through the orchard and by and by he came to a wood. There he caught sight of a farmer who was trying to make his pig climb up an oak tree. "What are you doing, my good man?" asked the lover. "I want my pig to eat some acorns," the farmer said, "but I can't get him to go up the tree." "If you were to climb up and shake down the acorns, the pig could pick them up," the lover said.

SPEAK "PIG . . ." AS IF YOU YOURSELF WERE AMAZED. LOVER IS OVERLY POLITE, TO HIDE HIS AMUSED DISBELIEF. HE HAS RECOVERED HIS TEMPER AFTER CONFRONTING THE LABORER. HE CONTINUES TO SPEAK OVERLY POLITELY AND ALSO SLOWLY.

"Why, I never thought of that," replied the farmer, who scurried up the tree. "Here is the second idiot," remarked the lover to himself.

PAUSE SLIGHTLY AFTER "WHY."

LOVER SPEAKS AS IF MUMBLING.

He followed a dirt road until he reached a poor hut. He noticed a pair of trousers fastened to the side of the hut and a bearded man who was jumping with all his might into the air so that he could hit the two legs of the trousers as he came down. "What is going on, sir?" the lover inquired. "This is the first pair of trousers I've ever had," whined the bearded man, "and I can't seem to get them on." "It would be much better if you held them up with your hands," explained the lover, "and then put your legs one after the other in each hole." "Dear me," said the bearded man, shaking his head, "you are sharper than I am for that never occurred to me." Then he took down the trousers and went inside to put them on. "Hmmm . . .," thought the lover. "I've succeeded in finding three people more foolish than my bride and her mother and father."

SPEAK VERY SLOWLY. MAYBE GESTURE: ONE HAND HELD UP FLAT FOR THE WALL AND THE OTHER HAND WITH TWO FINGERS POINTING DOWN TO REPRESENT LEGS, JUMPING AND TRYING TO FALL INTO TROUSER HOLES.

LOVER SPEAKS NATURALLY IN THIS EPISODE. HE IS CURIOUS AND HELPFUL.

LOVER SPEAKS SLOWLY AND THOUGHTFULLY.

MAYBE GESTURE, SHAKING YOUR HEAD WHILE YOU SAY "DEAR ME."

PAUSE SLIGHTLY BEFORE "HMMM. . . ." DRAW "HMMM . . ." OUT. MAYBE GESTURE, TWISTING YOUR FACE AS IF SUDDENLY THINKING OF SOMETHING.

With that, the lover went back and married the young woman. And, in the course of time, they had a great many children.

SPEAK RAPIDLY UNTIL END.

EMPHASIZE "MANY."

I like "The Six Sillies" because it is such a flexible story. You can invent different episodes of silliness each time you tell it; you can assume a variety of different attitudes about each character, according to your mood of the moment; and there are small environmental touches you can alter to suit particular circumstances. For example, if you or your listener are antialcohol, you can substitute cider or water for ale in the story. If you want the mother to perform a less typical activity than knitting, you can have her set down her hammer or her paintbrush when she goes to answer the knock at the door. If you feel the notion of names on a calendar is too obscure, you can have the daughter say something equally silly, like, "All the names I can think of are already taken."

The essence of the story, for me, is the "humanization" of the lover: his gradual approach toward assisting people who appear silly, rather than getting mad at them. For this reason, I prefer to have the laborer, the farmer, and the bearded man tell their dilemmas straightforwardly. All of us at some time have been equally as silly; and although I want my listeners to be entertained by the obvious silliness of the events I describe, I don't want them to scorn the perpetrators.

Depending on the situation, you may choose to begin a storytelling session that features "The Six Sillies" by talking about how, long ago, European villagers kept ale casks in their cellars and tapped them whenever a visitor came to call. Or you can talk about the custom of naming babies according to the names of saints on a calendar. Or you can just settle down and say, "Once upon a time . . ."

It is best not to make written notes in a book you may wish to share with others. If you possess some other written version of a story, however, either a manuscript you have created or a photocopy from a library book or a book you own, you can try choreographing a story in advance. You don't have to stick to the "script" you develop. The activity in itself will draw you closer to the tale and start you thinking about ways to interpret it vocally.

The main point of any preparation is to enable you to listen to your story before you tell it. If you don't actually practice it out loud or tape it and replay it for yourself, at least go through it mentally, as you wish to tell it, and pay attention to it with your "mind's ear."

The more you prepare in advance for storytelling, the better the experience is bound to be, for both you and your listener. How you prepare is entirely up to you, just as how you actually read a story to yourself (which is only partially determined by your facility with the language) is based on what seems important to you and what you yourself enjoy doing. Different tellers, different stories, different listeners, and different occasions can each invite different means of preparation.

Pathways To Storytelling

● Because professional storytellers have to project their tales in front of large groups, their delivery is much more emphatic and stylized than the delivery of the average amateur storyteller, who typically shares stories with a single listener or a very small group of listeners with whom he or she has a more intimate relationship. Nevertheless, you can learn much about how to lend variety to the pace and rhythm of your delivery by listening closely to live performances or recordings of professional storytellers. Among records that I have found particularly useful are Arthur Junaluska's *Navajo Bird Tales*, Swift Eagle's *The Pueblo Indians*, Jay Silverheels' *The Fire Plume*, and Diane Wolkstein's *Eskimo Stories* (all of which contain Indian tales); Ed Begley's *American Tall-Tale Animals*, J. Frank Dobie's *Southwestern Folk Tales*, and Ennis Rees' *The Song of Paul Bunyan and Tony Beaver* (all of which contain American stories); Pura Belpre's *Purez and Martina* and Augusta Baker's *Uncle Bouqui of Haiti* (both of which contain stories from the Caribbean); Christine Price's series of records featuring European tales (such as *Folk Tales and Legends from Great Britain* and *Russian Folk and Fairy Tales)*; Pearl Primus' *Africa;* and Harold Courlander's *Folk Tales from Indonesia*. Also look into Newberry Award–winning records and records of tales made by their authors (for example, those by Carl Sandburg).

● Most books about storytelling are full of tips regarding how to deliver a story effectively. Two good examples are Ramon R. Ross's *Storyteller* and Ruth Sawyer's *The Way of the Storyteller*. You may also want to consider taking a yoga course or an aerobics course to improve your breathing. As a bonus, such courses will help you concentrate and relax during occasions when you might otherwise be tense. Public-speaking courses can be of value for storytelling, teaching you a great deal about making your vocal delivery more interesting, even though what you are concerned about would be more properly called "private speaking."

● Just for fun, read Mark Twain's essay, "How to Tell a Story."

CHAPTER SEVEN

BEYOND STORYTELLING

I have always disliked the word *storytelling*. It is a makeshift word, closely resembling the terms George Orwell created for his ultrapractical, dehumanized "Newspeak" vocabulary in *1984*. I can understand, however, why a simpler, more evocative term did not evolve in the English language—or any other language I have investigated, for that matter—to describe the type of activity discussed in this book. After all, what we call "storytelling" encompasses so much that it defies an easy label. The "telling" part of the word touches on its most manifest aspect, but it also includes listening and reading and thinking and adapting and creating and caring and observing and planning.

Even more significant, however, is the fact that storytelling as a process has no clear parameters. It is not, strictly speaking, communication, or art, or recreation, but all of these and more. It constitutes a potential element in any form of human expression and can be incorporated into any encounter between two or more people.

What we have reviewed so far in this book is storytelling in its purest sense: the vocal transmission of a story from one person, identified as a "teller," to another person, identified as a "listener," who, because of the particular culture in which we live, is typically a child. But there are many other activities that feature storytelling elements and procedures besides the "pure" practice of storytelling. Depending on your lifestyle, personality, and interests you may consider them either as points of departure—things to do after you have mastered pure storytelling—or points of arrival—things to do that will lead you eventually to pure storytelling. Here is a summary of some of these activities:

Puppetry

Children love to play with puppets; but they are perhaps even more fascinated to see adults playing with puppets. Try dramatizing stories with puppets for your listener. The stories you choose should be very short and either full of talk (if you intend to have your puppet speak) or full of activity (if you intend to have your puppet remain mute).

Unfortunately, you are limited in the number of characters you can command. You can use either one puppet and act as a narrator, which requires a one-character tale; or two puppets—one for each hand—and act as a narrator, which requires a two-character tale; or two puppets and act as a third character, which requires a three-character tale that does not need a narrator.

The easiest thing to do with a puppet in terms of storytelling is to invent your own story and make yourself a character. Create a relationship between you and the puppet and set up a situation. Weave a tale through interacting in your own voice with the puppet, asking him, her, or it questions that will keep the story moving.

It takes more skill to be both the independent narrator of a story and the voice of a character-puppet. Many people prefer to keep a puppet mute and either to describe events the puppet acts out or to talk with a puppet in such a manner that the puppet's gestures and movements are sufficient response.

The best stories for puppets you will encounter will no doubt be the ones you yourself develop after getting to know a particular puppet well. The main idea behind puppetry is to be as simple and lively as possible, and you will be more spontaneous and free to ad-lib if the story you are presenting is your own. But there are numerous books available in libraries and bookstores that will provide you with story ideas: Look for them under the heading "puppets" or "puppetry." There are also books that will help you to construct your own puppets, which can be a lot of fun, especially if you involve children in your efforts.

When I was a kid, I used to entertain my little brother and the younger children in the block with stuffed animals. I gave each animal a distinctive personality and created stories around their interactions with each other, based on common, conflict-ridden themes of daily life and television sitcoms. My favorites were a bear (upbeat, agreeable, and conciliatory, if somewhat naive—like Mickey Mouse); a fox (imaginative, talky, short-tempered, and impulsive—like Donald Duck or Lucille Ball); a panda (loving, dumb, a follower—like Goofy); and an elephant (strong, silent, adventurous—like all the television western heroes). I gave them each a special voice and moved them around as they entered and exited what were essentially group scenes. Stuffed animals are not exactly puppets, but they can be used similarly for storytelling purposes. So can dolls, tin soldiers, ceramic angels—any objects meant to suggest humans or animals.

Drawing

If you enjoy sketching, you may want to execute a series of drawings to accompany a story you are telling a child. There are a number of approaches you can take: drawing each character as the character appears, drawing unusual objects as they are mentioned, or drawing different environments (buildings, landscapes, rooms) as they arise. You can sketch using a sheet of paper or a notebook, which your listener can keep, or using a blackboard.

Two of my favorite children's stories, "How the First Letter Was Written" and "How the Alphabet Was Made," both by Rudyard Kipling, literally beg to be drawn and require no particular drawing talent on the part of the teller. The former tale is about a little girl who attempts to create a written picture message for a foreign-speaking messenger to carry to her mother; the latter tale is about a little girl who winds up creating alphabet letters (like the ones we use) by sketching pictures of what she wants to represent. I leave the special delights of these two stories to your own discovery. They are as instructive as they are entertaining.

Many professional storytellers use a flannel board to illustrate their stories, and you may want to investigate making or purchasing one. It is merely a large, square board covered with flannel, to

Reading Aloud

Reading stories aloud to children is a wonderful way to teach them language skills and stimulate them to read more successfully and enjoyably on their own. It can never replace the intimacy and vitality of sharing stories face to face, but it is an important complement to such storytelling as it helps to make children more comfortable with the world of literature. Here are some tips for conducting this activity:

• Choose stories that have distinctive literary values. Compare different available versions of the same story and seek advice about individual story selections from source materials, librarians, teachers, and informed friends. Remember that a child's listening comprehension of syntax and vocabulary is far more extensive than his or her speaking or reading comprehension, so don't be afraid to pick challenging material—tales that will please your ear as well as your child's. The pleasure to be derived from hearing a well-written story does not stop after the child has begun reading independently. It is more likely, in fact, to increase.

• Practice reading aloud any story you are considering sharing with a child ahead of time. Make sure you know the meaning and pronunciation of words and that you can pace individual sentences so their meaning is clear and you do not falter in front of the child. Avoid any ad-libbing or editing when you are reading aloud. Children usually expect exactly the same story from a book every time it is read, and it is a good idea to give them this confidence regarding something in print. A story that has been composed by an author is one in which every word has been deliberately chosen to fit the whole. Mixing your own words into a work that is being communicated mainly in the language of someone else can create an awkward narrative.

• While you are reading aloud, assume a position that will allow you to make easy eye contact with your listener from time to time, so that you can gauge his or her reaction and so that the overall experience is more personal. If your listener is under ten years old, and still developing his or her reading-comprehension abilities, make sure that

he or she can easily follow the text visually as you read it.

• Experiment with different story genres, giving special attention to works the child may not be inclined to read on his or her own. Also try books with no pictures as well as books with a few pictures or a lot of pictures. Many readers find that pictures distract the listener's attention from what they are saying and prevent the listener from forming his or her own mental images; others like to pause in a story and converse for a moment informally with a listener regarding individual pictures.

• Bear in mind that by reading aloud from a book you are introducing a child to the physical book itself. You may want to purchase any book from which you read aloud so that you can lend it or give it to the child.

• First-rate guides for reading aloud, including many specific story and book recommendations, are Jim Trelease's *The Read-Aloud Handbook* and William F. Russell's *Classics to Read Aloud to Your Children*, both widely available in libraries and bookstores.

which felt cutout figures, designed to illustrate story characters, places, or objects, can adhere. If you are constructing your own board, try using foot-square tiles of indoor-outdoor carpeting, which works just as well as flannel and is easier to clean. Left on their own, children can re-create a story much more satisfactorily using a flannel board than they can drawing on paper, because the flannel board winds up looking just as it did when the story was told.

Speaking of children drawing pictures based on a story they have heard, I have found that suggesting such an activity to a child can work two ways: It can inspire a child to spend many happy moments creating works of art that are pleasing reminders of the story, or it can cause a child to feel pressured and confined and result in pictures that are disappointingly incapable of recalling the magic he or she experienced when the story was told. It all depends on the child and the occasion. Marie Shedlock offers a relevant anecdote in her book *The Art of the Storyteller*:

> I remember a kindergarten teacher saying that on one occasion, when she had told to the class a thrilling story of a knight, one of the children immediately asked for permission to draw a picture of him on the blackboard. So spontaneous a request could not, of course, be refused, and, full of assurance, the would-be artist began to give his impression of the knight's appearance. When the picture was finished, the child stood back for a moment to judge for himself of the result. He put down the chalk and said sadly: "And I *thought* he was so handsome."

I once dated a woman whose four-year-old daughter very much resented my intrusion into her and her mother's daily life. I was constantly looking for some way to win her over. She loved to draw, so I told her to draw a special picture for me and I would tell her a story about it. The picture (ironically?) was of a huge giant hovering over a little girl. It was not difficult to come up with "Jill and the Cornstalk." I think she appreciated my willingness to portray the giant as the one who gets defeated; and a tradition of a-picture-for-a-story was begun, with enthusiasm on both sides. You may want to establish a similar ritual with a child who you know likes to draw. Your story does not have to correspond exactly to a given picture. You can always pick out some detail and say, "That reminds me . . ."

Games

Children have a natural affinity for role-playing, and you may want to try acting out a story with a child. Dramatic playacting works best when you are alone with the child and unlikely to be disturbed for an extended period of time. Mutually determine what characters you will be.

Although you may end up sticking fairly close to the plot of a particular story, you will have more fun if you approach role-playing from the standpoint of embodying characters rather than enacting a story line. Make sure each character is very familiar to both of you and let the child express his or her desires first.

As you interact, let matters flow as they will. It is important not to insist that the characters behave as they do in the story from which they are derived and, at the same time, not to contradict intentionally the facts of that story. Be flexible and react naturally to your co-star. Chances are he or she will voluntarily keep fairly close to the story anyway. You can use props and costumes and designate any convenient item as either another character, a place, or a special object.

Many stories contain actual games within the context of their plots. This is especially true of formula tales. There is a whole subcategory of formula tales known as "finger-play" tales: "The Five Little Piggies" and "The Itsy Bitsy Spider" being perhaps the most familiar. Here is one that usually gets a warm response from a two- or three-year-old:

> Five little sausages
> Frying in a pan
> (hold up five outstretched fingers)
> All of a sudden
> One sausage went, "BAM!"
> (clap hands together)
> Four little sausages
> Frying in a pan
> (hold up four outstretched fingers)
> All of a sudden
> One sausage went, "BAM!"
> (clap hands together—proceed until
> all sausages are gone—then say):
> No little sausages

Frying in a pan
(shake head sadly)
All of a sudden
The PAN went "BAMMM!!"
(clap hands very loudly)

Just by making two of your fingers take a walk, you can create all sorts of simple "traveling" stories.

A librarian can help you find specific story games that will appeal to the age group and interests of your listener. Some stories imply games by having their characters perform unusual stunts. Does Fodor the Feckless have to learn to tie sailor's knots? You can get some diagrams and try those same knots with a child. Does Minnikin have to change himself into a fish? You and your child can pretend you are fish. It can be a game in itself simply to extract games from a story.

Creative Writing

Hearing a well-told tale can easily inspire school-age children to compose original stories in writing. Feel free to encourage your listener, well after the most recent storytelling session has passed, to try writing a story, either based on a tale he or she has already encountered or spun wholly out of his or her own experience or imagination. If a child knows you are interested, he or she will be all the more motivated to create.

Beginning writers frequently need a lot of encouragement and help; but just as frequently they are too independent to make a big issue of it. If a child comes to you for advice, offer any suggestions you wish: preferably a number of suggestions so that the child still has some power of choice. Probe to find out what interests the child and build on what you learn. Use some of the recommendations provided in the chapter of this book entitled "Creating Your Own Stories" and lead your listener to come to his or her own revelations.

Once the story is completed, ask the child to read it aloud to you, and praise its good points. Consider typing it out so that it looks substantial and impressive and so that you and your listener have copies. Maybe eventually he or she will want to tell it to someone.

Music

Many stories have their own internal songs. You can make up melodies and add these songs to the repertoire of songs you and your child possess. Songs work wondrously well in storytelling. They are especially rhythmic and memorable and a refreshing change of pace in the midst of a narrative. Because of this, consider working short songs into your own creative stories and repeating them—or parts of them—at appropriate points. Your listener may want to join in when you reach the song (a desire you can gently instill), which will involve him or her even more intensely in the story.

You can find many books in the library that not only feature stories with songs but also contain scores for those songs, enabling you to accompany your storytelling with music, whether you play a guitar, a banjo, an autoharp, a piano, a harp, or a lute. Also check into ballads, which are narrative stories in musical form, songs that are based on stories, and songs that have inspired stories.

Introduce your listener to musical comedies, operas, and ballets (either specifically geared to children or capable of holding their attention) by first telling them part of the story behind the music; or follow up such visits with related stories. You can also apply either (or both) of these procedures to movie or television productions.

One of the most engaging storytelling activities associated with music is to make up a tale to go with a particular piece of music that has no fully developed story of its own but merely hints at a plot, characters, and events. Kenny Rogers' "The Gambler," the traditional ballad "By the Banks of the Ohio," the camp song "John Jacob Jingleheimer Smith," and Michael Jackson's "Billie Jean" have all, at various times, given me not only story material but built-in refrains to add variety to my delivery.

Poetry

Many popular stories contain poems. Like music, poetry adds a pleasing variety to the pace of a story and can stimulate children to remember a tale more vividly. In certain cases, a poem will virtually encapsulate the whole tale or serve a major function in the plot or communicate the essence of the story more successfully than any other single aspect.

An outstanding way to give your listener a good ear for the language is to acquaint him or her with poetry you enjoy through the vehicle of storytelling. You can pursue a number of different routes: intentionally seeking stories that contain good poems, fashioning stories around poems you already know or create, or delivering poems that tell their own stories all by themselves.

I particularly enjoy doing the latter, especially when time is short for a storytelling session or when I need to bring a storytelling session to a quick end. Dip into *Mother Goose* and the works of Dr. Seuss for younger children, as a start. For school-age children, try the poetry of A. A. Milne, Carl Sandburg, James Whitcomb Riley, Robert Louis Stevenson, and Ogden Nash.

Excursions

Herman Storwick is a travel agent who has directed his passion for storytelling into a business he calls "New York Walkabout." He leads tours of people regularly along what was known before World War I as "Millionaire's Row"—Fifth Avenue between Seventy-eighth and Ninety-first Streets. "I invite you to use your imagination," he told one such group I attended. "The gutters are lined with cobblestone. Streetlights are gaslights. The air is perfumed with a sweet scent, and that is the sweet scent of money." He then proceeded to tell stories of the Vanderbilts, the Whitneys, the Mellons, the Fricks, and the Carnegies, all of whom once lived in buildings that still line the avenue.

You can borrow his idea and apply it to some of your favorite walks, describing events that actually occurred (or could have occurred) to a listener who is accompanying you. This works especially well when the listener is new to the area: on a vacation with you, visiting you, or just recently arriving to set down roots. It is uniquely meaningful for both of you when the area is your hometown or someplace where you spent a lot of time in the past.

Making Tapes

Listening critically to tapes of yourself spinning a tale is an invaluable means of improving your storytelling skills. It is also an invaluable means of providing your child with ongoing entertainment. If your listener possesses such a tape, he or she can summon up your image and relive the story whenever the moment seems right for it.

My mother lives a thousand miles away from her two grandchildren. But by sending them tapes of her telling a story, she can continue to be a living presence in their household between her visits. Tapes made by someone close can be a major consolation to a child who is left at home alone or with a babysitter.

If your listener enjoys telling stories, suggest that you record some of them and then make a copy of the tape to give to your listener. Your listener may be influenced to begin making tapes on his or her own.

Take care to separate any taping occasions from those occasions when you are actually telling a story to a child. Such a storytelling session is meant to be an "off the record" experience.

Jackie Torrence, one of the approximately 300 United States citizens currently earning their living solely by traveling from place to place telling stories, once remarked, "Many people think storytelling is weird. Somehow they think it's not a legitimate thing to do. It's like being a shepherd." Each time I recall this remark, I reaffirm my dislike for the term "storytelling." I partially blame its awkwardness for making the whole subject, and the people devoted to it, appear "weird." In reality, however, it is a sad commentary on the climate of the times that storytelling can appear weird. What, for that matter, is so weird about being a shepherd? Isn't some degree of "shepherding" involved in every human endeavor?

Whatever forms you decide storytelling will take in your life, you will be building on something that is already there. Creative storytelling, like creative living, is a matter of sharpening your observations and talents, committing yourself to that in which you believe, working in harmony with your own capabilities and the conditions in the world around you, and reaching out to others in a manner that is rewarding both to you and to them.

Pathways To Storytelling

Now that you have finished reading *Creative Storytelling*, here is an action plan you can follow to become a more effective storyteller. It calls for a one-month program, but you can easily adapt it to fit a smaller or larger span of time.

First week
• Recall stories you have heard or read in your life, particularly in your childhood, that have meant a lot to you. Jot down notes about them, taking care to articulate what it was that made them special. Try writing out the stories as you remember them. Then, look up and read written versions of these stories.

• Ask friends and relatives about stories they enjoyed when they were young. Have them recount these stories, and try to ascertain their sources. Look up and read written versions of these stories.

• Think of potential listeners you might entertain with a story—either actual children or children you can imagine encountering. Ask yourself, What stories, or kind of stories, would I tell these children?

Look up and read written versions of these stories.

• Keep a daily journal of your thoughts and observations regarding children and of any story ideas that occur to you.

Second week
• Acquire at least one collection of each of the different types of stories and read an assortment of stories in each collection. Make records of the stories you enjoy.

• Practice telling some of the stories you have read or heard or written out so far. Make records of your impressions based on doing this.

• Practice adapting some of the stories so that you have two or three possible versions of at least two or three stories.

• Continue keeping your journal about children and story ideas.

Third week
• Continue reading stories and practicing telling and adapting them.

• Using these stories as models, create some of your own stories.

• Practice telling one of the stories you have created and record your impressions of this experience.

• Continue keeping your journal about children and story ideas.

Fourth week
• Continue reading stories and practicing telling and adapting them.

• Using some of your journal story ideas, create some of your own stories.

• Practice telling one of the stories you have created and record your impressions of this experience.

• Plan at least two stories to tell to one of the specific listeners you considered during the first week (having two stories will ensure that you have a choice, a back-up, or an encore). Determine an appropriate time and place and think about how you will initiate and conclude the storytelling session.

AFTERWORD

STORYTELLING AND ENVIRONMENTALISM

The people of the earth have always had a special need for stories. Now the earth itself also has that special need. Since writing *Creative Storytelling*, I have noticed that storytellers who perform in public are increasingly drawn to stories that have environmentalism as a main theme.

Given how rapidly the earth is being polluted and debilitated, one might expect this trend among people who spend so much of their lives traveling the land and, as it were, living off the land's stories. But I'm convinced that other dynamics are equally responsible for this trend.

I believe that storytelling is a uniquely effective medium for motivating listeners and tellers alike to appreciate and to protect their natural environment. I also believe that crises of great magnitude, whether they are human-made crises or natural crises, cry out for the type of fresh, magical, heart-soothing and soul-stirring vision that only stories can provide.

Surely all of us must rise to the emerging challenge of preserving the earth instead of destroying it. And surely the earth today cries out anew for stories that offer symbolic expressions of its wonder and majesty, its power and vulnerability.

So much of the current appeal for greater environmental awareness is based on scientific arguments: the effects that specific toxins, waste materials, and energy coefficients may or may not have have on air, water, soil, and/or plant and animal life. Children certainly need to become better educated about these arguments; but a more pressing need, especially for children who are too young to grasp many of the relevant scientific principles, is the development of strong sensory, emotional, and imaginary ties to the environment.

Storytelling helps to weave such ties. And as children become more personally involved with the environment at this "non-scientific" level, they also become more receptive to the sheer aesthetic beauty of nature, and, ultimately, more responsive to scientific arguments about how this beauty came to be, why it is presently threatened, and what can be done to minimize or eliminate the threat.

With these sentiments in mind, let's consider how you can go about using storytelling to instill more environmental awareness in your young listeners:

Create stories that foster more environmental awareness.

The general objective of your made-up story can be any one or more of the following four goals:

(1) encouraging listeners to envision the beauty—and/or the despoilation—of the environment more vividly;

(2) counteracting harmful prejudices about the natural world (e.g., wolves and spiders are always "bad" animals; winter is always a "dead" season; storms are always "destructive;" wetlands and mud are always "yucky"; forests are always places where you get easily "lost" and encounter "dangerous" situations);

(3) influencing listeners to realize the interconnectedness of *all* aspects of nature (the so-called "web of life") and/or the interconnectedness of their *personal* lives with nature;

(4) inspiring listeners to take responsible action toward protecting the environment.

Here are some sample story ideas, each of which you can use as the basis for any type of tale you wish to invent— formula tale, fable or parable, fairy tale, folk tale, myth, legend, realistic adventure, or your personal type of story (also, see the suggestions given in Chapter Five, "Creating

Your Own Stories," especially on p. 134):

- the hero develops an adventurous relationship with an animal, a tree, or a positive (perhaps magical) individual who lives in a natural environment;

- the hero gets involved in a "science-fiction" or "magical" solution to an environmental problem or disaster;

- the hero learns (through self-help and/or the help of others) how to survive in an unfamiliar wilderness;

- the entire plot is told from the perspective of a real-life or imaginary animal, tree, or landscape;

- the hero has special powers that can be used to abuse or to benefit the natural environment;

- time travel shows the hero how human intervention caused a piece a natural paradise to degenerate into a wasteland—or vice versa;

- in an effort to solve a riddle or mystery, the hero learns some aspect of the food chain, such as ice cream made from milk coming from a cow eating grass;

- an environment-saving mission shows the hero how recycling works and what happens when there is no recycling;

- the accidental or engineered disappearance of a particular animal, plant, or natural element shows the hero its importance to the environment (e.g., getting rid of mosquitoes in a pond leads to fish starvation, bird disappearance, etc.);

- the plot reveals how a particular plant, animal, characteristic of a plant or animal, or a natural feature came to be.

Tell or adapt existing stories that foster environmental awareness.

Do some investigation on your own in the children's section

of commercial bookstores and libraries, and be sure to ask bookstore managers, librarians, day-care center personnel, and teachers for their suggestions. Environmental groups and organizations (some of which are listed further below) may also be able to recommend specific stories, authors, or story collections. Other possible sources are bookstores—or story-telling programs—at a zoo, an aquarium, a national or state park, a nature preserve, or a natural history museum.

Native American stories are especially good for fostering environmental awareness, not only because of the close bond between Native American cultures and the land, but also because that land is the land which all residents of the United States now share. I particularly recommend an anthology of Native American stories entitled *Keepers of the Earth* (Golden, CO: Fulcrum, Inc., 1988). Put together by Michael J. Caduto, an ecologist and storyteller, and Joseph Bruchac, a poet, novelist, and storyteller of Native American ancestry, *Keepers of the Earth* combines Native American stories with related environmental activities that children and adults can perform together, or that children can perform on their own.

Be creative in your hunt for good stories. Some stories and story collections are not necessarily well-known for promoting environmental awareness, and yet they do deliver symbolically important environmental messages to their readers. Among works of this type that immediately come to mind are: Dr. Seuss's *The Lorax*, which stirs up empathy for many aspects of nature—animals, trees, water, and land; Shel Silverstein's *The Giving Tree*, which explores the multi-faceted relationship between a tree and a growing child; Ruth Krauss's *The Carrot Seed*, which helps very young children to appreciate the planting cycle; and a Readers' Digest collection entitled *Animals Can Be Almost Human*, which contains 82 real-life tales of animal behavior that can easily charm children into thinking of animals more compassionately and respectfully.

Also, try telling stories (existing ones or invented ones) that feature famous fictional characters or real-life people who are closely associated with nature. Possible fictional characters to consider include Doctor Doolittle, the crusading veterinarian in Hugh Loftis's entertaining series of books; Hans Christian Andersen's the Little Mermaid, who always retains her love for the sea; and Jim Henson's number one Muppet, Kermit the Frog, who is ever concerned about the well-being of his "hometown" swamp. Possible real-life people include St. Francis, the founder of a Roman Catholic fraternal order who revered all living creatures; Johnny Appleseed (aka John Chapman), the wandering planter who lived with the creatures of the great mid-American forest; and Jane Goodall or Diane Fossey, each of whom developed marvelously close relationships with primates in the African jungle.

As an alternative to telling stories that use famous fictional characters or real-life people as heroes, try telling stories with heroes that are similar to these characters or people. Make up your own version of Doctor Doolittle, Kermit the Frog, Johnny Appleseed, or Diane Fossey and use this hero in story after story after story.

Finally, keep abreast of environmental stories in the news: efforts to preserve the habitat of an endangered species, to clean up a waste-strewn neighborhood, to rescue an animal that is stranded in a life-threatening environment, or to influence developers to design projects that are more environmentally sound. These stories can often be translated into very dramatic, informative, and inspirational tales.

Create, or take advantage of, appropriate opportunities for telling stories with an environmental theme.

Among the more obvious occasions for such stories are during a camping trip (especially around a well-controlled campfire), or during a nature hike (when storytelling can provide a doubly refreshing break), or during a trip to any natural environment—beach, desert, mountain, or forest— that is unfamiliar to the listener. Other occasions to consider, however, are visits to a farm, a zoo, an aquarium, a museum, a park, a nature preserve, or any nearby environment that is somehow threatened, or has the potential to be threatened or has already been changed for the worse, by human intervention. Your environmental story does not have to address the particular locale or situation at hand, although it will be even more compelling and memorable if it does.

Also, consider the appropriateness of particular *times* as well as *places*. For example, you might mark the occurrence of a full moon, or an equinox, or a change of season, or a major storm with an appropriate story related to environmentalism; or you might tell a story related to a specific environmentalist issue that is currently prominent in the news.

Above all, you will want to make the most of times when a child expresses a particular interest in some issue related to environmentalism. Whether that interest manifests itself as a simple question, such as "Why is the sky blue?," or as an ongoing concern, such as tending a garden or collecting insects, take it as an invitation to tell a story that will encourage your already receptive child to be even more sensitive toward that particular aspect of nature.

Involve children in spinning their own stories related to environmental issues.

Children frequently enjoy inventing their own "tell-aloud" stories on the spot, whether that spot is their bed, the living room floor, the backyard, the front seat of the car, or a campfire site. One of the best ways to stimulate this type of storytelling is to make a game of it, either by starting the story yourself and letting the child finish it, or by taking turns with the child in advancing the story (so called "participatory storytelling," as described on p. 147). In its April/May 1988 issue, *Children and Animals* magazine printed some excellent story-starters relating to environmentalism. Here is a sampling:

for younger children (stories that involve make-believe animals):

- I am the last purple parrot. I live in a zoo. But I remember what life was like in the jungle. I was free to fly wherever I wanted.... .

- A rainbow lizard! For a scientist like me, this is a real find! Maybe it is the last one in the world. Still, it seems a shame to catch it. Maybe I should let it stay free. What's that noise? Someone's coming....

- "There used to be lots of long-tailed squirrels," said my Dad. "But now they are found only in one place...in the forest on Mrs. Johnson's land. She's going to sell her land. A shopping center will be built there. That will be the end of the squirrels," said Dad. "Maybe I could talk to Mrs. Johnson," I thought. There had to be a way to save that land.

for older children (stories that involve real-life endangered animals):

- **Gorilla**: The jungle was quiet. The only noise came from birds in the trees high above. Suddenly there was a loud crash. Men were shouting at one another. I ran as fast as I could. I climbed a tree trunk and watched the men below. I had just escaped being caught in a huge net. But my mother had not escaped. The men were pulling the net off her. She struggled and tried to bite them. But it was no use. They put her in a large crate. Where were they taking her?....

- **Pelican**: The fish tasted funny, but I was hungry. So I ate it anyway. Then I saw that all around me there was a scum on the water. It smelled terrible. Down on the shore, a man was wading in the water. He kept shaking his head sadly. I went back to the shore. Some of the other pelicans were there. Many of them were sick or weak. "I hope I don't get that way," I thought, as I ate another one of those funny-tasting fish.

- **Tiger**: I could hear the poachers talking as they neared my hiding place. "If we could just bag that tiger!" said one. "We could really use the money we'll make from selling its hide." They were getting closer. The other one raised his gun. "What is that hiding in the tall grass?" he asked. He was looking right at me... .

Become more informed about environmental issues and about how children can—and do—take active roles in promoting environmentalism.

Start by paying closer attention to environmental stories in local newspapers and newscasts, by investigating magazines and books related to environmentalism at your local library, and by contacting local organizations with a special interest in environmentalism (from Girl Scout and Boy Scout groups, to city and/or state departments of parks and/or conservation, to citizens' committees on specific issues). As you develop more familiarity and interest in a particular topic, pursue it on a more far-ranging level. To reverse a favorite environmentalist slogan, "Act locally, then think globally." In addition to *Keepers of the Earth,* mentioned above, here are some other books for children on environmental topics that I especially recommend:

Earthworks Group, *50 Simple Things Kids Can Do to Save the Earth* (NY: Andrews & McMeel 1990);

MacEachern, *Save Our Planet* (NY: Dell, 1990);

Hollender, *How to Make the World a Better Place* (NY: Quill/ Morrow, 1990).

Here are some national organizations that are especially helpful in providing environmental information, contacts, and activity suggestions:

- Children's Rainforest: P.O.Box 936, Lewiston, ME 04240 (particularly interested in educating children about, and involving children in protecting, the Costa Rican rainforest);

- Greenpeace USA: 1436 U Street NW, Washington, DC 20009 (the United States branch of an international activist organization committed to all facets of environmentalism);

- National Audubon Society: 950 Third Avenue, New York City, NY 10022 (a private organization that publishes a nature magazine dedicated to environmentalist principles and that promotes environmentalist causes of all types in the United States);

- Renew America: 1400 16th Street NW, Washington, DC 20036 (a promotional organization that collects and supplies up-to-date information on a wide variety of local, state, and national environmental groups, programs, and issues);

- Tree People: 12601 Mulholland Drive, Beverly Hills, CA 90201 (an action group committed to planting and preserving trees, with a particularly strong outreach to children).

Obviously, the more well-informed you become about environmental topics, the more ideas and material you will have to tell stories with environmental themes. However, always remember that it is far more vital to communicate the fundamental spirit of environmentalism than it is to communicate facts associated with environmentalism. This is especially true in the context of storytelling.

Don't ever think that you must have facts, or that you must deal with scientific rationality when you tell stories designed to encourage environmentalism. A story told to a child may include actual facts—and, if it does, it can be a great vehicle for enhancing a child's real-life education; but it certainly does not need to include facts to inspire a child to be a more thoughtful steward of the world in which he or she lives.

Indeed, whether or not an individual story contains real-life facts, storytelling as an experience always and inevitably offers a subtle freedom from the world of real-life facts. This freedom serves a very important function when it comes to telling stories with environmentalist themes. However significant the facts associated with environmentalism may be, these facts in themselves are simply too confining, too limited, and too lifeless to invoke the true wonder and life-force that is the very essence of the natural world.

Once William James, the famous American scientist and philosopher, lectured on the latest scientific theories about the origin of the universe to an audience that included a Native American woman. After James' lecture, the woman told him a creation story from her own culture. It ended with the earth riding on the back of a turtle. Reacting somewhat defensively, James said, "Madam, I find your story very interesting, but one point is hard for me to reconcile: If the Earth is supported by the turtle, then what is it that holds the turtle up?"

"Why, another turtle, Mr. James," she replied.

"But don't you see that there would be nothing to hold up the second turtle, or the one beneath it?" he pressed.

"I'm sorry, Mr. James," she answered. "But it's turtles all the way down."

Such is the nature of nature—an endless mystery no matter how deeply we look into it. And such is the nature of storytelling, always working to remind us that the human heart has a mind of its own, and that the human mind must likewise have a heart.